LOVEJOY
ON FOOTBALL

Tim Lovejoy was born on 28th March 1968. He presented *Soccer AM* for a decade, making it into a Saturday morning institution. He now presents *Something for the Weekend* and *Soccer USA* and is a presenter on Radio Five Live 606. He supports Chelsea FC.

LOVEJOY

ON FOOTBALL

TIM LOVEJOY

arrow books

Published in the United Kingdom by Arrow Books in 2008

1 3 5 7 9 10 8 6 4 2

Copyright © Tim Lovejoy, 2007

Tim Lovejoy has asserted his right under the Copyright, Designs and Patents Act 1988
to be identified as the author of this work

First published in the United Kingdom in 2007 by Century
Random House, 20 Vauxhall Bridge Road, London SW1V 2SA

Arrow Books
The Random House Group Limited
20 Vauxhall Bridge Road, London, SW1V 2SA

Addresses for companies within The Random House Group Limited can be found at:
www.randomhouse.co.uk/offices.htm

The Random House Group Limited Reg. No. 954009

www.rbooks.co.uk

A CIP catalogue record for this book is available from the British Library

ISBN 9780099519591

The Random House Group Limited supports The Forest Stewardship Council (FSC),
the leading international forest certification organisation. All our titles that are printed on
Greenpeace approved FSC certified paper carry the FSC logo. Our paper procurement
policy can be found at www.rbooks.co.uk/environment

Design & make up by Roger Walker

Printed in the UK by CPI Bookmarque, Croydon, CR0 4TD

I dedicate this book to my brother James.
Without him introducing me to The Specials,
I might have been a New Romantic.

CONTENTS

Prologue 3

1 **Let football into your life** 7

2 **Never trust someone who hates football** 19
Five reasons why I, Timothy Paul Lovejoy,
    am a rubbish football fan
Getting my first pair of boots
My first replica kit
Looking good, feeling great
Why football clouds my judgement

3 **Modern football irritants** 33
Turning the tables
The England band
Mascots
Mascots II
The minute's applause
Shadows on the pitch
Lookalikes
Undersoil heating
Choreographed goal celebrations
The fourth official's board

Manager's technical areas
PR people
The songs they play at matches
Half-time 'entertainment'
Three substitutes
Player ratings
Football chat rooms
Booing
Player cam
Streakers
Pundits

4 What I've given to the game 49
The 'Save Chip' phenomenon
Ridiculous theories
Kicking a ball through a hole
The bouncebackability campaign
The Sven waxwork
Bodybuilding for the common man
Easy, easy!
The star on the England shirt
The fans of the week
Showboating
The nutmeg files and taxi
The crew
Thank you and goodbye

5 Lovejoy's Legends 71
Mickey Thomas
Frank Worthington

Robbie Savage
Jimmy Bullard
Gerry Armstrong
John Terry
Robbie Fowler
Neil Ruddock
Carlton Palmer
Luther Blissett
Chris Kamara
Paul Gascoigne
Charlie Nicholas
Tim Lovejoy

6 If you're gonna go (here's what you must know) 87
Choose your seat carefully
Know your silverware
Establish a rapport with rival fans
Learn to loathe rugby
You must be superstitious
Always, always, always hate the most successful team
Make sure you know the words to your club's songs
Don't be afraid to do a u-turn
Don't believe what other fans tell you
Embrace new technology (and use it to annoy your mates)
Enjoy every moment
If all else fails, give up

7 Women in football. Discuss 109
The trouble with women's football
Never let children near your treasured possessions

Treat the missus well
Not all women are the same
Toot camp
Women + T-shirt x football = soccerette
Why there will never be a female referee
She's the boss

8 **The power of television** 119

Blood Ray Parlour...
Star Quality
Table for two
Early doors
Razor's revenge
Anthony Hutton killed celebrity football
There's no business like showbusiness

9 **Referees I Love** 133

10 **Unwritten rules of football** 135

11 **Bring on the Badgers!** 145

My penalty hell
The badgers – where are they now?

12 **Managers** 155

Alex Ferguson
Gordan Strachan
Ian Holloway
Harry Redknapp
Jose Mourinho

Kevin Keegan
Neil Warnock
Barry Fry
Being a manager is easy!

13 Lovejoy's on his way to Wembley (and other notable football stadiums) 169

The greatest goal I never scored
Stadiums I have (dis)graced
My favourite dressing room
A New Wembley

14 Bloody foreigners . . . I love 'em! 179

Welcome to England!
View to a skill
Glove story
Stick with what I know
Boys will be boys
When in Rome . . .
ZZ Tops
My favourite ever player (in theory)

15 Once upon a time in America 197

16 There'll always be an England 209

Shoot!
Bring back the dentist's chair
The problem with England songs
Why white?
Sing your hearts out

Come together
Managing expectations

17 Why nothing beats playing football 221
Ball watching
Deep down I still think I've got it

18 Hard fought lessons of a football fan 231
Don't hate glory hunters
Understand that home advantage is claptrap
The 1980s
Don't be afraid to follow other clubs
The colour of your kit is key

19 Money: the root of all brilliance 249
Young at heart
Shirt changed
Tap tap tap ...
By loyal appointment
TV, quick!
Give your chairman a break
This is war ...

Epilogue: What I still have to do to become the biggest fan in the world 267
I have to see England win the World Cup
I need to watch a football match in every continent
I have to meet Pele and Maradona
I have to father a son who can play professionally
I have to own my own football club

LOVEJOY
ON
FOOTBALL

PROLOGUE

'WHO DO YOU SUPPORT?'

Whenever you're asked this question in the back of your mind you're getting ready to justify how true a fan you are:

> 'I've been going since I was five . . .'
>
> 'My grandad's originally from the city . . .'
>
> 'My dad made me . . .'
>
> 'It was the first match I saw on TV . . .'
>
> 'It was the first Panini sticker team I finished . . .'

People having to justify who they support is my eternal bugbear with being a football fan. Football is for everyone, and being a fan has been taken over by what I like to call football fundamentalists, who have adopted the term 'real fan' and used it to spread fear amongst the normal football-loving man. These people are always miserable and always trying to find reasons to drag football down, whether it be money, foreigners, ticket prices or board takeovers. I'm obsessed with football, but they're obsessed with proving they're obsessed about football.

3

Football in my opinion is the most important subject in the world. It's the true world sport and the one thing that unites every nation (well, apart from America).

And let's remember, we invented the sport, so let's rejoice in it and enjoy it for what it is – the best game to ever grace this planet.

I don't want to rant but I'm going to anyway. We need to reclaim our national game from the fanatics, 'real fans', and give it back to the people. I'm by no means the world's biggest Chelsea fan, but I am a massive fan of football and in my world whether you go to away games or not, or go at all, or whether your team's the other end of the country or just up the road, or even whether you've never owned the club's shirt, or you've got the club crest tattooed all over your body, to me it's all irrelevant. I believe being a football fan ISN'T about:

Stats;

Never missing a match;

Trying to prove you're a bigger fan than the next man;

Or moaning about how the game was better in the past.

What it IS about is:

Enjoying watching football, whether it be on the terraces, TV, or YouTube;

Engaging in banter with mates down the pub;

Kicking a football at any opportunity;

And being miserable when your team gets knocked out on penalties.

This book is a combination of memoirs and opinions, and I hope as you're reading it you'll disagree with loads of stuff I say, because that's what football really is all about. No one really understands everything about the game, but everyone thinks they're an expert. But as I say, when it comes to football I might not always be right...but I'm never wrong. Oh, and forgive me when I indulge myself in this book and go off on the occasional tangent, but this is the first time I've written a book. I'm sure J.K. Rowling's s******g herself.

The great thing about this book is how many people have written to me saying how they now fit in as a fan. I was right that I share that feeling that I'm not a real fan with many of you. Whether it's a Liverpool fan from Norwich or an Arsenal fan from Southampton people realised. In fact this book got great reviews from everyone apart from a couple of football magazines who trade on the old fashioned 'real fan' ideals. However, these magazines don't sell enough copies to fill Spotland (Rochdale's stadium) so it doesn't matter what they think.

1

LET FOOTBALL INTO YOUR LIFE

religion: the belief in a superhuman controlling power, esp. in a personal God or gods entitled to obedience and worship. 2 the expression of this in worship. 3 a particular system of faith and worship.

A friend of mine who's an artist is always saying, football has no relevance, no culture. We've wasted many hours arguing over this. She's of the belief that football is for uncouth morons who spend their afternoons getting drunk and singing songs, and hurling abuse at everyone.

This is
true.

But it's not called the beautiful game for nothing. Is there anything more breathtaking than watching a player like Barcelona's Lionel Messi dance through the Getafe defence? For the millions of people who watched that clip on YouTube, it's like a religious experience.

I have never been religious. As far as I can gather church services have always tended to be on Sunday morning and that, I'm afraid, was when I was out playing football. Faced with such a dilemma (OK, not that much of a dilemma) there was only ever going to be one winner.

Football is the nearest thing I have had in my life to a religious enitity. It is an ever-present force for good in my and many other people's lives. It is, perhaps, the only constant I have. If I am depressed or down, football will lift my spirits. It has and continues to play a massive part in enriching my life. It has always been there for me and I know it always will.

Now take a step back and ask yourself if you like football in any way, shape or form. If you can answer yes then this book is for you. If you said no then bear with me because I really want you to think again. In fact, I want to offer you salvation. Don't worry if you don't consider yourself a real fan. Don't worry if you have never even been to a game. I want to present to you a game that welcomes each and every one of you.

Rewind a number of years to a pointless conversation I had sometime with a fellow Chelsea fan. There we were talking about the relative merits of some player or other when he piped up with 'But you don't even go to away matches. What would you know?' Correct me if I'm wrong but how on earth does that affect my opinion on football? Why does travelling up to Middlesbrough or Sunderland or Blackburn mean you know more than me? Does it really mean that just because you go to away matches in faraway towns you are a bigger and, therefore, better football fan than me? Of course it doesn't. Now, whenever I'm challenged on the subject I tell people that I go away all the time but only if it's to Rome, Monaco, Barcelona or somewhere else equally glamorous in the Champions' League.

OK, so I may know only a few facts and figures about Chelsea, but that's because my memory is like a sieve, not because I don't care or because I don't enjoy the game as much as the next man or woman. It's the same with music. I love music passionately but can I name every album or single there's ever been? 'Oh you don't have the entire back catalogue of Pink Floyd?' Well, no I don't but so what? I still like music. Stop trying to test me you bloody fascist bully. Let me get on and enjoy it.

And that's the way it should be. You should enjoy football in whatever way you want. I may not know who scored Chelsea's winner in the 2-1 away win Arsenal in 1976 but I do know the difference between a good player and bad player, between good tactics and bad tactics, between good managers and bad managers. Don't get me wrong, a lot of people out there derive a great deal of pleasure out of facts and figures and the history of the game and that's great. I don't. I'm not a stats nut. But that doesn't make them a better a football fan than me, does it?

I have never been one of those people that wallows in nostalgia. The thing I get excited about is the here and now and the future. When the season ends, for example, I count the days until the fixture list for the next season comes out and when the fixture list is released I count the days until the season starts. But when someone says, 'Do you remember that League Cup tie four years ago?' I'm like 'No, I'm really sorry but I don't remember anything.' So I've got a rotten memory. Does that make me a fraud? Does that make me a fake fan? Of course not.

That was one of the reasons we got such great guests on *Soccer AM* because we never set out to make people feel uncomfortable. Often, they would come on and say 'I'm not really a football fan so don't ask me too many questions about football' and why? Because they were petrified of being outed as something other than an all-knowing encyclopaedia of the game.

There are too many nob-ends out there willing to criticise those who enjoy their football in any way that isn't the week in, week out, spend every waking hour and every last penny you've got manner of following your team.

That's wrong. Whether you watch it on telly, go to matches home and away or go to one match every ten years, it doesn't actually matter. Who cares if you only got into football after Euro 96? Who cares if you only supported Man Utd because they had David Beckham? Who cares if you don't know who won the World Cup in 1938? It doesn't matter. What does matter is at least you finally found football. At least you have been born again.

When I started presenting *Soccer AM* on Sky Sports I thought I was going to be outed as a 'fake' fan and started worrying about my football supporting credentials. I didn't 'go away' anymore, I was playing Saturday football so I didn't have a season ticket, I couldn't name all the 1955 championship winning team. In fact I couldn't name any of them at the time and what's more I didn't care. This used to make me wake up in cold sweats, then one day it came to me, that warm glow of comfort that I was a football fan and I was not a charlatan. I just loved football and that was all there was to it. I have played or watched football every week of my life since a ball was put at my feet and that, my friends, is proof enough to myself that I'm in love with the beautiful game.

Once you've found football and let it into your life it will be with you forever. Even if you're reading this and you've never seen a game in your life, I urge you to come and join those of us that have opened our hearts to football. This is our religion, our faith. Think about it. Football imposes no restrictions on your life. It offers complete freedom of expression and freedom of choice. There's no brainwashing, no donations, no fairy tales, no prayers (well, not many) and no guilt. What other religion offers you that?

And I would go further than that. The way I see it football is more important than politics too. After all, can you show me anything else that has so much power over the people of the world? It's also a stereotype, but also true, that football unites people. Recently Iraqis celebrated winning the Asian Cup – and people normally at each other's throats were out celebrating in the streets together. You want more proof? OK, how many member states are there in the United Nations? I'll tell you. There's 192. Now, how many countries do you think tried to qualify for the last world cup? I'll tell you again – 198. It's an amazing statistic and one that, arguably, makes the FIFA President Sepp Blatter, and not Dubya, the most powerful man on the planet.

The truth is the whole world plays football and it is the only thing that unites the entire world. Wars, conflicts, disputes; everything stops for football. More people listen to footballers speak than they ever do to Presidents or Prime Ministers. And while those in the arts world may regard the game as uncouth, it is played in every single country in the world. Moreover, it is a real indication of a country's soul. Brazilians, for instance, are said to play with the rhythm of the samba, the Latin countries play with flair and passion and the British teams possess that never say die spirit. These may be stereotypes but they're undeniably true. That's why I think David Beckham going to the Los Angeles Galaxy could be a fantastic move because if he can get the United States into football – really into football – then the last major nation to resist the game will have been conquered. The rest of the world, meanwhile, are already addicted to the game. From Asia to Africa, South America to Europe, China, Australia, everyone has taken on football. It is the number one sport in the world by miles and it always will be. I remember going to Vietnam on holiday once and as I was taking a ride in a rickshaw, the bloke driving turned round and even though he couldn't speak any English he said 'Arsenal?' When I told him I was a Chelsea fan, he said 'Dennis Wise! Ruud Gullit!' It's the same anywhere. My grandad has always believed that football is the best way to start a conversation with a stranger. Just ask them what team they support and you're off and running.

It was on the same trip to Vietman that I had conclusive proof that football was, by some way, the biggest single thing on this planet. Me and my girlfriend (and future wife) had taken a trip up a mountain on the back of a couple of mopeds when we got chased by these menacing looking blokes who were also on mopeds and off their heads on rice wine or something and wielding knives and swinging punches. It was very scary. Even our guides were shaking and that's never a good sign. They pursued us down mountain tracks for fifteen minutes, but it seemed like hours, as the moped slid from side to side, avoiding low-hanging branches and holding onto my guide for dear life. Eventually we managed to get away from them but by the time we got to the bottom of the mountain one of the bikes had a flat tyre. As we looked for help we came across a little village so we asked about to see if anyone could repair it and we were shown to a little shack where this woman ushered us into this very little room. There in front of me were the entire family all sat around a basic television watching France v Japan. So I sat down and watched it with them, and after being chased down a mountain by maniacs who wanted to kill us, there I was now in a house in the middle of nowhere with a strange cup of tea watching the football and everything was alright with the world again.

After an hour or so, the guides came back in and said the bike was fixed and we could get going again. But there was ten minutes left so I thought what the hell, Zizou was playing. I sat back down, had another cup of tea and carried on watching the match. That's the beauty of football. You try watching any other programme in a foreign country and you won't have a clue what's going on. But football? It's a universal language.

Some of my friends only watch football on TV but they're just as passionate as I am so I have full respect for them. Football is the greatest TV experience: it has the good, the bad, the joy and the tears. It's reality at its finest: Gazza's tears, Beckham's free kick against Greece or Cantona's Kung Fu attack. You can't script that sort of stuff. It's better than any soap.

It's true, football brings joy to a great many people across the world. And, personally, I know the wonderful effect it can have on people going through bad times. When my brother was very ill with cancer, I used to go round to his house and we would talk for ages about football and it always cheered him up. As kids we had gone to Watford games together and when he managed to get himself well enough to go to Vicarage Road and see a game again he was so excited. For him, it felt like he was on the mend. But he wasn't. He died soon after at the age of 37 and at the next home game at Watford they put an obituary in the programme for him. He would have loved that.

2

NEVER TRUST SOMEONE WHO HATES FOOTBALL

I always advise girlfriends of mine, when they're looking for potential partners, to make sure they ask the man what football team he supports. It's irrelevant who they do support, but if they are into football in any small way, it's a starting place for realising they're halfway normal, and you have a decent chance of a relationship.

I've made a lot of friends through football – playing, watching and talking about football, and I know it's clichéd, but it really is the best ice-breaker between two men. I remember my first day at Cassio college in Watford (one of the few I bothered to turn up to), I was really nervous as I didn't know anyone. I was stood next to a bloke called Andy Butler and he said, 'Who do you support?' I said 'Chelsea, what about you?' He replied, 'Forest,' and from that moment on respect was established and we've been friends ever since. This story has been repeated continually throughout my life with many of my friendships established through conversations about football: Ben (Southampton), Mike (Chelsea), Andy (Man Utd), Barry (AFC Wimbledon), Dougie (Celtic), Dave (Arsenal), Neil (Chelsea), Richard (Leeds), Simon (Barnsley), Shandy (Arsenal), Chip (Coventry), Joe, Ryan, Paul and Leon (all Chelsea), Rick (was Arsenal, now Chesterfield?) . . . I really could go on forever.

So, this is the story of how I became a football fan . . .

I've never checked but as far as I'm aware everybody in

Northwood, Middlesex supports Chelsea Football Club. Being born there, I suppose I had no choice either. I guess I started following them when I was three, although I'm not entirely sure why. If anything it probably had a lot to do with the song 'Blue Is The Colour'. My mum and dad bought me that record and I played it to death. For a while, I even thought Chelsea was a man and not a team. When my dad sat me down and explained that he was actually an it, I was disappointed and still a little confused.

Back then, all my family seemed to talk about was football. I remember my dad and my granddad sitting down every week and watching the highlights on *The Big Match* on Sunday afternoon. They'd get incredibly animated and really over-excited by the whole event. It was one of those quintessentially male things of sitting round together and watching the football. It was a rite of passage, if anything.

But then I was no different to every other boy in Northwood. All I ever wanted to be was a footballer and to play for Chelsea and for England. There was no other career for me. All or nothing. Somehow, though, I slipped through the net. Even when we moved to Rickmansworth (near Watford) I never got spotted. I played for my school team, St Clement Danes, a comprehensive in Chorleywood, and I like to think I was Chorleywood's answer to Roy Keane. Sadly, growing up in the Watford area meant we ended up imitating the local professional team. In our case, that meant wingers and long balls. It was percentage football. Win the ball and get it up the field. The scouts, it seems, never made it as far as Chorleywood. Inner Watford maybe, but not the football hotbed of Chorleywood. Looking back, Watford Football Club should be ashamed of themselves. Think of the revenue they could have made when they sold me to Milan in the 1980s. Think of the shirt sales, the merchandise, and their slice of my image rights. Heads should have rolled.

It was while I was at St Clement Danes that I thought I'd better go to my first club football match. Me and my brother pleaded with my dad to take us. For years, he'd said we weren't old enough, but now as a teenager, surely the time was right. As you know, I was a Chelsea fan, and my brother had leanings towards Spurs at the time, so when my dad said he was going to take us to a match, we got really excited. Was it going to be Stamford Bridge, or White Hart Lane? No. It was going to be Vicarage Road, home of Fourth Division Watford. We wanted to go to the terracing, but my dad made us sit in the Shrodells stand. I can't remember who Watford played, but still, I was hooked. Watching live football was my drug.

I had many happy days watching Watford. I would play football for the school in the morning, and me and my brother would take the tube or the bus to the ground, and we progressed from the Shrodells into watching football on the terraces, and I even bought a replica Watford shirt. I actually celebrated Watford's promotion one year by going fully-clothed in the pond at the top of the high street with a thousand other Watford fans. My brother and me missed the last bus, and had to walk home thoroughly wet, trying to think up excuses for our mum as to why our Doc Martens were soaked through.

Having been to games at Fourth Division Watford, watching players like Ross Jenkins and Kenny Jackett, the time had come to go to Stamford Bridge and watch my first love, Chelsea. It was like another world. When you came out of Fulham Broadway tube station, you would turn left and then the sheer enormity of the occasion would just hit you. I'd never seen anything like it. Don't get me wrong, Watford was a brilliant club but there was something magical about the atmosphere at Stamford Bridge. There were thousands and thousands of fans. There were ugly, menacing skinheads, scores of huge police horses and an atmosphere unlike anything I had ever experienced. The smells, the noise, the colour; I was hooked.

Soon, I started going to Stamford Bridge every week. This was the era of Micky Droy and Johnny Bumstead, Kerry Dixon and David Speedie, and managers like Bobby Campbell, John Hollins and John Neal. To be honest, going to Chelsea back then had less to do with the actual football and everything to do with the atmosphere. It genuinely felt like I was an integral part of the football club and that I belonged to something. Football was everything to me. I played Saturdays and Sundays and then went training Tuesdays and Thursdays. I used to go home and away with Chelsea and only stopped going when I was playing football. Nothing got in the way of my football.

Nothing.

Even when Chelsea weren't playing I used to look at the other fixtures and just go to a game. I remember going to Spurs v Aston Villa at White Hart Lane simply because I wanted to see the likes of Gary Shaw and Glenn Hoddle play. In those days, you didn't need a ticket weeks in advance, you could just turn up and pay on the turnstile. The trouble with that was that being a Londoner I couldn't exactly go in the Villa end so I had to go in the Spurs end and then feign delight when they scored so as not to attract attention. That's not easy, especially when you don't really care.

Things have changed though. As you can see, I am absolutely obsessed with football, but according to the laws of being a football fan, I'm rubbish. Let me explain…

FIVE REASONS WHY I, TIMOTHY PAUL LOVEJOY, AM A RUBBISH FOOTBALL FAN

1 **I used to go and watch Watford before I watched Chelsea.**
There is no long Lovejoy family line of Chelsea fans going back into the mists of time, although there is one for Spurs and Arsenal. In fact, my dad supports both of them. That's right, Spurs AND Arsenal. He lived up Highbury way and his defence is that he is simply a fan of football so he went to whoever was playing at home that week, which is fair enough I suppose. My dad gets annoyed with me, not for being a Chelsea fan, but during matches which are neutral, his theory is that I should always support the London team first, followed by the team from the South, then the Midlands, and finally, right down the bottom of the pecking order, is any team from the North (especially the North West). I don't play his game – I support who I want regardless of location to my birthplace. When we're watching football together, my granddad likes to wind us up by supporting Man Utd, if Arsenal aren't playing, and always supports the foreign team over the English team. I can't wait until I can also be a grumpy old man who always goes against the trends to wind everyone up.

So I'm rubbish because I'm the only Chelsea fan; it's not like it was passed down from generation to generation. That said, I am trying to start a new family line of Chelsea fans. I've been doing my utmost to make my daughters support Chelsea but sadly my ex-wife has somehow managed to turn them into

Swansea fans. So now I'm fighting back. My latest plan is to convince them that Cardiff City is in fact the team to support. It's like some horrible mental game we're playing with our daughters' minds. Still, they'll get over it.

2 **I don't go away any more.**
According to football fan law, fans who don't travel away with their club are not fans at all. These days I don't go away, again proving I'm rubbish. Actually, that's not strictly true. I do still go to the occasional Chelsea away fixture but only if it involves going on a plane to somewhere exotic to watch them in the latter stages of the Champions' League, like Rome, Monaco or Barcelona. If you're going to do it, you may as well make the most of it. Still, you've got to admire the fans that spend all their time and money following their teams week in week out but I can't do that any more, especially when you've got kids to indoctrinate.

3 **I have no memory for facts and figures.**
I have the most shocking memory when it comes to football. It's actually appalling. And it's not like I go to a game and don't pay attention. Quite the opposite. When I'm at a match I am utterly transfixed and absolutely enjoy every single second of it. But if you try and pin me down on when Chelsea won a particular trophy I really couldn't tell you. Yes, I can name the years of the League titles we've won but that's not exactly difficult when you've only won three of them, is it? In that respect I would be the world's worst Liverpool fan. For some reason, if you support Liverpool you have to know every single fact and figure about every single match ever played, ever, otherwise you're nothing. I'm not sure quite how many of them actually know who the

manager was before Bill Shankly, but there's no doubting they're by far the most obsessive fans when it comes to facts and figures that you'll ever meet. An example of this is my mate James Redmond, the actor from Hollyoaks and Casualty. I met him at a party when he was modelling. I said to him, 'Who do you support?' He answered, 'Liverpool. Who do you support?' I said, 'Chelsea.' Again, from that moment on, we've been friends. He knows everything there is to know about Liverpool. In fact, he stayed round my house a few times and on Saturday afternoon, after the final whistle, he sits down with a book, writes out the results, team line-ups, and stats from the Liverpool matches, and commits them to memory. He really is the ultimate Liverpool fan.

4 I don't sing any more.

However I am the biggest hypocrite because there's nothing I like better than a great atmosphere, proving once more I'm a rubbish football fan. It may be an age thing but I just can't do it. Back in the 80s, at the height of my casual days, I'd join in with all the classics. My favourite songs were the ones unique to Chelsea, like 'Celery' and 'One Man Went to Mow'. However, I always cheated when it came to that last one. For anyone who doesn't know, it's a committed song that takes a good five minutes to get through, starting at 'One man mowing a meadow…' and finishes with everyone standing up in the all-seater stadium singing, 'Ten men went to mow.' I used to start at seven or eight and take the glory at ten. Hats off to those who made it all the way through.

5 I don't want to win at all costs.

I don't agree with the old adage, 'Win at all costs.' Some people think that if you play ugly football, as long as you take the three points, that's ok. I just want to see great football all the time. That's why I don't like it when the opposition's best players are out with injury or suspension. I want to see the best eleven against the best eleven. I want to see my team beat the other team without any excuses. Say I'm going to watch Chelsea play Man Utd and news breaks that Cristiano Ronaldo is out with an injury. A lot of people I know will be rubbing their hands with glee. I won't. I'll be gutted because I'm missing out on the opportunity to watch a great player in action. This could potentially cost us three points, which again is why I'm a rubbish fan.

So there are the five reasons why I'm apparently a rubbish fan. Or am I? Let's rewind a bit here and see where my football obsession grew from, and where it apparently all went wrong…

GETTING MY FIRST PAIR OF BOOTS

As well as watching football, playing has always been an important part of my life, and nothing was more important than getting my first pair of boots.

But what kind of football boot I had was a constant bone of contention in our house. I always wanted proper screw-in studs but Dad made me get moulded studs because he reckoned they would last longer. It's bizarre, because nowadays all I ever want to do is play in moulds because you get a better touch and feel for the ball.

The day I got my first pair of Adidas World Cups was possibly the most exciting day of my life. They were my dream boot, and a timeless classic, which are still loved by the pros today. I'm a size nine, and I bought them size eight-and-a-half, like I'd read in the magazines that all the pros did. I took them straight home, ran a bath, laced them up, and climbed in so the leather would stretch round my feet, so I could get the perfect touch and feel on the ball. My mum was never impressed with me sitting in the bath with my football boots on, but it had to be done. As impressive as the World Cups were, the trouble with them is they didn't seem to last long, especially when you're playing every day, so I ended up buying their biggest rival, and the only boot on par with the World Cups, the Puma King, which stood me in good stead.

Times have changed now. Today's kids have different studs for different surfaces. When I was younger you had one pair of boots and that was it. It didn't matter if the pitch was frozen or waterlogged, you were playing in studs and that was that. What's more you'd keep wearing them until the studs had all but worn away and you couldn't get them out again. Finally, when I got older, I bought myself two pairs of boots. That's when you know you've made it.

During my playing career I became very interested in boots that they only used on the Continent. I owned Pantofola d'Oros, Valsport Greenstars, and at the moment I'm playing in a pair of £280 pearl-coloured Hummel Professionals that are the most expensive boots in the world. Fortunately I got them for free working on *Soccer AM* because that's a lot of money for a boot. My playing days are coming to an end but still to this day I can't walk past a sport shop without having a look-in to see if they've got any new boots on offer.

MY **FIRST** REPLICA KIT

Kids don't know how lucky they are these days (I've always wanted to say that). When I was a young kid, there was no such thing as a replica football kit. Your mum had to sew a badge onto a shirt that was a similar colour (see the picture of me in a 'Chelsea' tracksuit). But replica kits came shortly after and the first football shirt I got was the England kit from around 1982.

It was the white Admiral one with red and blue panels across the tops of the chest and England wore it at the World Cup in Spain. My mum and dad bought it for me for my birthday but I wasn't allowed to wear it outside until my actual birthday and so it sat in my room in a box for what seemed like eternity. It was torture. Every night, I used to smell it or try it on in the mirror, thinking about what everybody would say when I finally went out in it. When my birthday finally arrived I practically lived in that shirt.

Still to this day I love football kits. The first thing I do in the morning is put on a pair of football shorts to walk round the house in. I have everything from Madrid and Juventus to Boca Juniors. I'm sad to say, the running theme in pictures of me throughout the time, especially on holidays, is I'm generally wearing a replica football kit.

LOOKING GOOD, FEELING GREAT

Going to football is not just about watching the action, it's also about making sure you're dressed right. Back in the 1980s, it was actually more of a fashion show than anything else. We were all casuals and looking good and wearing the right gear was absolutely imperative. I had a big blond wedge, a haircut that I honestly believed to be the best wedge in Hertfordshire. I still remember taking a photograph of the Aston Villa player Gary

Shaw into the hairdressers and asking for the same wedge as him and then coming out thinking I was the business.

I loved my hair. I used every lotion and potion to keep it in tip-top condition; gel, mousse, hairspray, anything that kept it looking just right. I used to have the blondest highlights I could get. But in those days it wasn't as easy as now. They hadn't invented foil highlights. I had to sit with a swimming cap on my head which had holes in it, and the girl from the salon had a long knitting-needle style thing, which she used to dig into your scalp and pull out through the hole. But the pain was worth it to look good.

But it wasn't just the hair. The clothes were equally important. I had to wear the right trainers (Diadora Bjorn Borg Elite, if you must know), the right Lois Jeans (frayed) or Lois jumbo cords (split up the sides to sit on the trainer correctly), a Kappa or Lacoste t-shirt covered with a Sergio Tacchini tracksuit top. Other brands that I used to wear on a Saturday were Pringle, Lyle & Scott, Fila, Giorgio Armani and also the classic Benetton rugby shirt. Clothes were a massive part of my life and I had a few tricks of the trade to make me look like I had a bigger wardrobe than I really did. Firstly, I would always leave the labels in tracksuit tops, and wear them out for a few times then take them back to the shop, say I didn't like it, and change it for another colour. You could do this for about three times with each one before they sussed it. The other trick was that I used to buy a pair of Lacoste socks, cut the crocodile off, and stick it on a plain polo shirt.

It didn't end there. I used to cover myself from head to toe in jewellery, from rope-chains to belchers. I was a walking Ratners. I even had both of my ears pierced. For some reason, whenever I left the house to go to the match, my dad used to wolf whistle me.

WHY FOOTBALL CLOUDS MY JUDGEMENT

Looking back I realise how ridiculously important football had become in my life at the time. Saturday was the day I lived for and being a casual, I'd sometimes leave early for the match and stop off at Stewart's in Shepherd's Bush to look at the new Tacchini tracksuits or maybe head to Piccadilly Circus and spend a few hours in Lillywhites looking at gear I couldn't really afford.

One Saturday in December 1983 I decided to go to Harrods to look at their clothes instead. As I still had some time to kill before kick-off I asked the doorman if he knew where the Pringle shop was so he gave me these directions and off I went in search of some quality knitwear. Half an hour later, though, I still couldn't find the place so I went back to Harrods to check with him. Once again, he told me and off I went. Just as I was walking round the corner, though, there was this almighty explosion.

It was pandemonium. People were crying and screaming and, suddenly, all you could hear was police sirens. When I got to Knightsbridge tube station, a policeman told me they'd closed it and all I could say was, 'But I've got to get to Chelsea!' Everyone around was in this blind panic. I was completely oblivious to the fact that an IRA car bomb had just killed six people and injured countless others. All I could think was that I'd arranged to meet my friends in the pub and I was going to miss them. Remember, there were no mobile phones back then, and tracking them down would have been a nightmare. Some people who've had close shaves like that have flashbacks or nightmares, but not me. It's never really bothered me as to how close I was to being caught in that bomb. All I was concerned about was that it had completely mucked up going to Chelsea.

There was an even more extreme example of my football obsession when Princess Diana died in 1997. Me and Fenners from *Soccer AM* and his mate Stanny had gone out the night before and woke up in my flat in Ladbroke Grove excited about watching Newcastle v Liverpool on the TV. I walked into the front room where Stanny told us that Lady Diana had died and they were cancelling the match as a mark of respect. We were horrified. That fixture had become one of the matches of the season and we were all set for enjoying another classic. We just couldn't comprehend why they had to cancel the football. From our point of view, there seemed to be no logic in it. It simply hadn't occurred to us that to many people Diana was this iconic figure who had tragically passed away. Only later did I realise how stupid I was to think that match was so important.

But that's football. Girls come and go, jobs come and go, friends come and go but football is a constant. Watching it, playing it, talking about it. I often ask myself what I'd be doing if football didn't exist. I haven't yet found an answer to that one. Doubt I ever will.

3

MODERN
FOOTBALL
IRRITANTS

An important part of being a football fan is you have to have a moan. This is what makes British people great – the ability to whinge more than any other nation. However I believe that football fundamentalists or 'real fans' are moaning about the wrong things. Basically they don't like change; if they had their way, football would not have moved on from the 1950s and you'd still be allowed to commit GBH on a goalkeeper to score a goal. I'm one of these people who embraces changes, football is better than it's ever been, even though I still look back fondly at the era of terracing. But being an Englishman I do like to moan, and these are the things that I don't like in the modern game.

TURNING
→ THE TABLES

There is one issue in football that annoys me above all others and that is the way that they've systematically mucked around with the names of the divisions. It. Does. My. Head. In.

Things have moved on dramatically since the formation of the Premiership in 1992, so much so, in fact, that the Premiership isn't even the Premiership any more. Oh no, it's 'The Premiership'. You see, I liked the old names – Division 1, Division 2, Division 3, Division 4. It just seemed to be the natural order of things, not just in England but everywhere else too. In Italy, for example, they have Serie A, Serie B, Serie C and so on. It's simple, it's easily understood and it works. Just like it used to here.

When the First Division ended and the Premiership came into being it took me a while to adapt but gradually I got there and began to accept the new order: Premiership, First Division, Second Division and Third Division. Then, just as I was getting comfortable with that the old Second Division became the Championship, the old Third Division became League One and the old Fourth Division became League Two. Now, not only had the names changed but they're also a 'League' and not a division any more. Got that? Me neither.

Consequently, anybody of a certain age has to explain league placings in terms of 'the old Second Division' or 'the old Third Division' because they haven't really got a clue what's going on any more. The only people that benefited from the changes were those teams in 'the old Fourth Division'. Suddenly, without ever doing enough to earn promotion they found themselves two divisions better off.

All these pointless changes have also made the ugly phrase 'top flight' into one of the most overused terms in the game. So now rather than explain that it's been so many years since Liverpool won either the First Division title or the Premiership version, they say 'it's been 17 years since Liverpool won the top flight'.

It's also worked wonders for Sky television too in that by forming an entirely new league, there was now a whole new set of records to be made and broken. Forget Dixie Dean's scoring record, all that mattered now was the all-time highest scorer in the Premiership. Now, there's every Premiership record under the sun; most clean sheets, most corners, highest jumper, whitest teeth. Truth is, these are all nonsense records because believe it or not, football in England didn't begin in 1992.

THE **ENGLAND** BAND

The 'England Band' send me insane in the brain. If you didn't know, the band is basically a bunch of really nice blokes from Sheffield who also play at Hillsborough for Sheffield Wednesday games. They came along at a time when the atmosphere at England games wasn't at its best and when it needed a little lift and for a while it worked. This, I seem to recall, was about ten years ago, when we all decided that the only way forward for England supporters was to pretend that we were really Brazilian and that meant having a band, or at the very least, a drum and a trumpet. I think we had all seen the Italian fans with their enormous drums and decided that as we were back in European competition again, we needed to adopt a more modern, continental approach to supporting our teams and that, sadly, meant getting our own amateur musicians in.

For a while, the idea of the band seemed to work; we even featured them on *Soccer AM*. In fact there was football band mania at one stage when every team in the country had someone turn up with some sort of instrument from a snare drum to a flute. Helen Chamberlain used to take a drum to Torquay and we regularly featured the killjoy clubs that banned her from taking her drum on Saturday mornings.

But as time has worn on they've really begun to try my nerves, not because they're terrible people – they're not – but because (a) I once sat within a couple of rows of them at an England match and only when you've done that do you finally realise just how painful the England Band experience really is on your ears, and (b) because their repertoire is a little limited. Think about it. What have they got? They've got The Great Escape, they've got Rule Britannia and maybe Land of Hope and Glory. Oh and they've also got a comedy party piece too. Whenever the physio runs on to the pitch to treat an injury, their trumpeter goes 'Nee-nor, nee-nor, nee-nor' in an attempt to sound like an ambulance siren.

I don't want to criticise the band because they are all genuinely nice blokes, but it's now out of fashion and I think we should get rid of the band and take the atmosphere in a different direction. Failing that, they should at least get some girls in bikinis with them to do the samba, otherwise what is the point? By the way at this point we should all feel a little sorry for Portsmouth fans who have to listen to a bloke ring a bell for 90 minutes each week. It must be like Chinese water torture.

MASCOTS

Whose idea was it to have 22 mascots being led out by the teams, instead of just the one lucky kid that it's always been and why has no one ever questioned it? Now at the start of any big game, there's a mascot for each and every player, which, by my reckoning, means that once you've included the four match officials and the TV crew there are well over 50 people waiting in the tunnel. Do we really believe this is helping kick racism out of football?

MASCOTS II

Men and women in furry costumes? I actually quite liked them till I went to America and watched theirs. In the good old US of A they wear a furry costume whilst doing acrobatics, flick flacking down basketball courts or round baseball squares. These are genuinely talented people who amaze you with their stunts, sadly our furry suits contain fellas who can only wave and hand out sweets. That doesn't annoy me, but what really does get on my nerves is that they have some sort of painful *It's a Knockout*-style race every year. Who, apart from Stuart Hall, actually thinks this is entertaining?

THE MINUTE'S APPLAUSE

A strange thing happened at the FA Cup Final this year. No, not Chelsea winning, but the minute's silence at the beginning of the game for the late Alan Ball. Well, I say a minute's silence but it was, for the first time ever in English football cup final, a minute's applause, just like they do on the continent. Don't get me wrong, it was entirely fitting that we all remembered one of England's greatest ever players this way but to be honest, I still prefer the old minute's silence. Sure, you'd occasionally get the drunk and disorderly ruining it or someone's mobile phone going off, prompting a vicious backlash from everyone else in the stand but people did tend to observe them quite well, didn't they? I was told that when Princess Diana died, they had a minute's silence for her at an England game soon after. In the post-match press conference afterwards, Glenn Hoddle was asked about it and he said that he had never heard a minute's silence like that before.

Brilliant. The way I see it, having a minute's silence is a great way to start a game. Well, OK, maybe it's not that great because someone has died after all, but it certainly helps to create a buzz around the ground. There is something unique about the end of the minute's silence that as soon as the referee blew his whistle to mark the end of it, there would be this enormous roar, the adrenaline would kick in and you knew the match was about to begin. It was like the calm before the storm.

SHADOWS ON THE PITCH

Every season we see new stadia appear. One thing I can't understand is with all the great architects and huge amounts of money that is supposedly being spent on these sporting temples, why is it that no one's worked out a way of stopping half the pitch being in sunlight and half the pitch being in shadow? This is fine for the fans who were actually at the match, but for anyone watching it on television, the camera has to keep changing its white balance so we can try and make out the ball. Clearly in the North West people don't have to worry about this because it's always raining, but a message to the rest of the chairmen: if you are building a stadium, why not work out where the sun rises and falls and where the shadows will affect the game.

LOOKALIKES

Every newspaper, magazine and website now has a 'funny' football section, which are varying degrees of funny. Sadly, a lot of them have the same thing – Ginger XI, Fat XI, Bad Haircuts XI and so on. But the worst crime has to be Football Look-alikes. I have always said that you are running out of material when you start doing look-a-likes and I stand by that.

UNDERSOIL HEATING

Undersoil heating is rubbish. OK, that may be overdoing it but these days we never have any snow on the pitch and that's a crying shame. You might think it's good to never have any games called off from frozen pitches, but the down side is it means we never get to see the orange ball of yesteryear and it also means that you never see scores of volunteers turning up to games with shovels to clear the pitch at 2.30pm.

CHOREOGRAPHED GOAL CELEBRATIONS

You know the kind of nonsense. Players re-enacting favourite scenes from the DVD they watched on the team bus, players cradling imaginary babies or choreographed dance routines commonplace in the lower leagues. My favourite celebrations have always been the simpler, more natural kind where the player just runs off excitedly into the distance, like Alan Shearer or that aeroplane/crucifix thing that David Beckham or Alan Smith do. The only other ones I can tolerate are the multiple flick flacks on a greasy surface ending in an impressive somersault. But my favourite goal celebration of all time has to be the Mickey Channon Windmill. In fact, it used to be my default celebration when I played for my team, The Badgers. It's a classic. You just put the ball in the back of the net and then wheel away, windmilling your arm. Beautiful.

PROPER ENGLISH

Has the word 'those' been taken out of the footballer dictionary, as it never seems to be used in post or pre-match interviews by anyone connected with football? Instead, it's always replaced for the word 'them'. I don't want to turn into an English teacher but it annoys me so much that wherever they're from in the country they have to use 'them' instead of 'those', for example, 'them goals', 'them players', 'them fixtures'. It's not complicated, it's only basic English.

THE FOURTH OFFICIAL'S BOARD

Part of the fun of going to football was never knowing exactly when the game was going to end. Cue mass whistling from the crowd ten minutes before the end as a gentle reminder to the ref. The uncertainty over when the final whistle would blow created a real atmosphere of suspense. Now we've scoreboards that tell you exactly how many minutes have been played, and the fourth official's board, which indicates how much injury time is left, there's no guessing left. It also stops players running up to the ref in the ninety-first minute wanting to know how long before he blows his whistle, and the crowd guessing from the ref's body language. No one can forget the last match of the 1988/89 season, when Steve McMahon asked the ref how long left there was, and then proceeded to tell all the Liverpool players 'Just one minute,' only for Michael Thomas to go up the other end and score, winning the title for Arsenal.

MANAGER'S TECHNICAL AREAS

Why are coaches only allowed within the confines of that tiny little box? As far as I'm concerned, managers should be allowed to go wherever they want; right along the touchline, behind the goals, even on the pitch if they really need to. Besides, they never really stay in their technical areas anyway, do they? You watch. Whenever they can, they'll always venture over the dotted line, just like their players when they're trying to steal an extra yard or two at a free-kick. Then, when they get ordered back by the fourth official, they'll retreat, only to do it again five minutes later. They can't help themselves. But I suppose it gives the fourth official something to do other than hold up a board.

PR PEOPLE

I like the fact that football has got more commercial. I think it's great that big money wants to associate with it, but with big bucks comes PR people. There are some good ones but they equate to about 1 percent of the entire PR industry. Sadly, a lot of the ones I've dealt with know diddly squat about football fans. An example of this is when you achieve a certain level of celebrity, you tend to get offered a lot of lucrative jobs. Trouble is most of them are rubbish. Recently, some PR company or other had the bright idea of me doing some promotional work wherein I would go around the country on Saturday and take to the nation's pitches to talk to the fans. As if. Now, whoever came up with this idea clearly knows sod all about football because as soon as I went on any pitch the ground would be drowned out with chants of 'Lovejoy Is A

W✱✱✱✱✱' or some such. In fact, I would have no respect for them as fans if they didn't abuse me. In the end, I explained to them that all they would be doing, effectively, is paying me a lot of money to be verbally abused every Saturday. I might as well become a ref.

THE SONGS THEY PLAY AT MATCHES

It's bad enough playing 'We Are The Champions' every time a team wins a trophy but what's worse is the trend for clubs to play songs whenever their team scores. Invariably, it's something like James Brown's 'I Feel Good' or 'Glad All Over' by the Dave Clark Five. Whatever it is, it's not good. It's like the Mexican wave.

MEXICAN WAVE

Rubbish. Fine for sports like athletics and grid iron, but I have no respect for anyone who has time to watch the wave come round readying themselves to stand up and throw their hands in the air. Why aren't they watching the bloomin' match? It's also the ultimate insult to the players on the pitch as it basically says 'you're not entertaining us!'

HALF-TIME 'ENTERTAINMENT'

I'm all for football evolving but certain new developments just make me angry. You see, there was a time when all you ever got at half-time was a few records played over the pubic address system and a quick run through the rest of the latest scores from around the country. That, along with a drink, a snack and a trip to the gents, was all you ever really needed.

Today, there's all manner of stuff going on at half-time, stuff, I should add, that nobody in the crowd gives a monkey's about. There's no-mark pop stars plugging their singles, penalty shoot-outs, five-a-side games, raffles, mascots; the list goes on and on. Truth is the best half time entertainment is either a penalty shoot out from two local schools or even better some ground staff armed with forks, fixing the pitch for the second half.

When I used to go and watch Watford they were always trying to liven things up at half-time. You'd be standing there minding your own business when all of a sudden some bloke would come flying in on a parachute and land in the centre circle. The biggest crime when it comes to half-time 'entertainment', though, is any club that employs the services of a troupe of cheerleaders. Cheerleaders are a uniquely American phenomenon and should be seen inside on a basketball court or, if outside, in sunnier climes, such as LA or Dallas – not a freezing cold Tuesday night in East London.

3 SUBSTITUTES

Being allowed three substitutes means that the nation's fans are robbed of the opportunity of seeing a badly injured central defender limping around up front for the last ten minutes of the game just because the permitted one substitute had already been brought on. Also we're often robbed of seeing one of the outfield players pulling on the keeper's shirt and getting bombarded by long range shots.

PLAYER RATINGS

If you're like me you'll find yourself casting your eye over the ratings the newspapers give the players. But to be honest, I think the whole thing is a farce. I remember one England game against Andorra when our goalkeeper Paul Robinson must have touched the ball once in the entire 90 minutes. The following day, one paper gave him 7 out of 10 while another gave him 6. How does that work? Surely he should have got 10 out of 10 on the basis that everything he did was executed perfectly and England didn't concede any goals? What was he expected to do? Come out of his goal and score a hat-trick?

Where do people get off with booing their teams? I don't remember fans booing their own players at half time and the end of every match years ago. Obviously you booed the opponent, but never your own team as a whole. I will go on record now as saying I've never booed Chelsea and I never will. When we were crap for all those years I never booed us, even though I had every reason to. These days, you only have to have one bad game and everybody is on your back. You'll be booed onto the pitch, booed off it at half time, booed back on to it and unless you get the right result, booed off it at the end of it as well. Does anybody really think that professional players really go on to a football pitch with the express intention of not giving it their all? Of course they don't. Yes, it's your right as a paying spectator to voice your disapproval but if you're going to do it each and every time you watch your team, then what is the point in actually going to the game in the first place? Save your boos for the referees.

FOOTBALL **CHAT**ROOMS

When these first arrived I started reading them, even taking them seriously, and I genuinely used to take offence at any comments aimed at me, my show, or my football team. However, over the years I've thought about what sort of people write on them and I can tell you it's not people like me or my friends, it's probably not people like you reading this either. It's fine to have an occasional dabble in them, a little read, maybe the odd comment to wind someone up. But the people who are on there all day, every day, are the ones that trouble me. They clearly don't have a life and I imagine the average profile of them is either angry fourteen-year-old boys or fat, sweaty bachelors who switch between that and some grubby porn site all day.

PLAYER **CAM**

Since Sky took over the rights to the domestic game there has been an explosion in the technology used to cover football. Generally, a lot of it works but PlayerCam was nonsense. My main problem with it was that the cameras were always too tight on the player in question and you never got any idea of where the player was on the pitch or where he was in relation to the ball. The other issue was that it was always the box office players that were chosen. It was never your workhorse centre-half or your veteran left-back. It was always Gerrard or Lampard, Henry or Rooney. It was never Frank Sinclair.

While we're on the subject of bad camerawork, I also hate it when there is a bit of a ruck going on and every player on the pitch is looking at it but the director isn't. I, the viewer, demand to see what they're seeing. I demand to see the action.

STREAKERS

There are two types of streakers: good ones (women) and bad ones (men). Sadly it's more men than women who seem to do it these days. That said, I applaud television directors who refuse to show male streakers running around on the pitch, especially that really irritating Scouse bloke who does it at every sports event he can. Doesn't he realise that nobody finds it funny, and everybody in the entire world hates him for doing it?

PUNDITS

When it comes to pundits, I have a hard and fast rule I always apply and that is that I will listen to those people who have been there and done it, like Alan Shearer and Ruud Gullit but I will not entertain those ex-players who have fallen into a media career and openly criticise something they have no direct experience of. How can they comment on England at the World Cup? Did they ever play in one? I don't think so. And while we're on the point, why are so many of them so negative about everything? Even before England have stepped out on the pitch at a major tournament, they should be on the plane home. Maybe if we were more positive about them they would stand a better chance?

I like line-ups full of experience for what they're talking about. Take Sky's Champions' League coverage. They've got Gullit, Wilkins, Souness, Hoddle – all great players who know the game inside out and expertly anchored by Richard Keys. I had a go at Keysie's job for the Carling Cup last year and while it was great fun, it was really difficult. He makes it look effortless which just shows you what a pro he is. Mind you, I would like to have another go at it one day and do it my way.

Another addition to Sky's team sheet has been Jamie Redknapp. He's a key appointment. Often you have too many pudits who are very good at analysing a game but who have not been in touch with the players for years. Redknapp's different. He's only just retired and knows the players involved. He's played with them. That's a big plus. That seems to be the policy that Setanta are employing now as well. They've gone with a team including Steve Macmanaman, Tim Sherwood and Sir Les Ferdinand and it makes a refreshing change from having to listen to some ex-manager or other who last played in the 1970s.

Incidentally, I had a chat with Ruud Gullit once while I was at Sky. He said to me: 'Hey Tim, are you still doing that little show on Saturday morning?'

'Yes,' I said.

'You know, we used to have a show a lot like that in Italy when I was at Milan…' he continued.

'Really?' I said.

'Yeah,' he shrugged, 'It was like yours…but it was funny…'

Got to love that man.

4

WHAT I'VE GIVEN TO THE GAME

When I was a kid Saturday revolved around football. Come to think of it, it still does. You'd get up, play football, come home, watch *Football Focus* or *Saint and Greavsie*, go out and play football and then come in for the vidiprinter and Final Score.

For me, the best day was always FA Cup Final day. I'd wake up in the morning, switch on the telly at 9 o'clock and settle down for the build-up to this huge match. And it was a *huge* match. Back then, the build-up went on for hours and hours. It was absolutely brilliant. There would be visits to the teams' hotels, you'd see maybe the Man City team eating their Cup Final breakfast or Spurs boarding their bus. There would be Tarby or Stan Boardman cracking gags on the team coach, you'd hear the Cup Final songs and see the teams being measured up for their suits. It was utterly compelling.

That was the thinking behind *Soccer AM*. I wanted to try and create a football programme that provided the same kind of build-up, the same kind of anticipation to the focal point of the football fan's day, which is obviously kick-off at 3 o'clock. I like to think we achieved that.

Part of the appeal of the show was that it had a very inclusive feel about it. Everyone who watched or featured on the programme was treated the same, regardless of whether they were season ticket holders or armchair fans. The material was always really strong too. How do I know? Because I once met an advertising executive who said to me. 'You know what Tim? We all love watching *Soccer AM*, because we can just sit there, watch the show, rip all the great ideas off and then stick them in an advert . . .'

To begin with, *Soccer AM* was all about mimicking football fan culture. But as the seasons went on, we began to have an effect on the actual culture that we built the show around. We also had an influence on the way football was presented. When I produced *Soccer AM* ten years ago, goal highlights always had to have either commentary or, if you were going to put any clips to music, the words of the song had to correlate with the pictures. For instance, overused tracks included 'Jump Around' by The House of Pain, Republica's 'Ready to Go', Kool & The Gang, 'Celebration' and nonsense like Queen's 'We Are The Champions' (which I hasten to add, is *still* used whenever a team wins a trophy. Please, if you are a tannoy man and reading this, on behalf of football fans everywhere, could you never play this again). Anyway, I decided to simply put great goals with great music and not worry about the lyrics. People at Sky worried about us doing this initially, but as time has shown, football and music go hand in hand, and this formula has been replicated countless times since.

THE 'SAVE CHIP' PHENOMENON

Everyone loves a campaign. Sadly, there are precious few campaigns that are actually worth getting behind these days. That said, *Soccer AM*'s 'Save Chip' campaign was definitely one worth backing.

It all started with me phoning up my mate Chip one day just as a really big game of football was on the telly. As we were speaking, I could hear *Coronation Street* in the background and as I knew he only possessed one TV set I asked him why he wasn't watching the match. 'It's not my turn,' he said. 'I've had my ration this week.'

It transpired that Chip had cut a deal with his partner Sarah that he could have a subscription to Sky Sports on the condition that he was only allowed to watch one live football match each week, in addition to watching *Soccer AM* on a Saturday. When I heard this, I was flabbergasted. It was like Chip was being denied his basic human rights. It was plain wrong. So whenever we read out the live games on TV that week on *Soccer AM* I started to plead with Sarah live on air to let Chip watch a few more games every week. This went on for a few weeks until one day when we started doing it again, somebody just shouted out 'Save Chip! Don't let Sarah win!' Robbie Knox, better known as The Tramp, swears he invented this, and although none of us knows for sure whether he did, he's not a liar, so I'm going to give him the credit.

Anyway, that was it. From that day, the 'Save Chip' campaign just snowballed. It was incredible, not least because it means bugger all in the grand scheme of things. What it did do, though, was stir into action all those people who knew exactly how Chip felt. They empathised with his plight and wanted to get involved. They wanted their right to watch football as and when they wanted.

Eventually, we decided to make some 'Save Chip' packs to send out and distribute at all the football grounds across the country. These consisted of a badge, a poster and a car sticker. Once we mentioned them on the show, we were flooded with letters from people wanting one. It was an absolute nightmare. We had to get in two work experience people just to send out packs each week. Before we knew it there were 'Save Chip' signs everywhere you looked and not just at the football. You would drive down the road and there would be 'Save Chip' stickers in the back of cars or 'Save Chip' written into the dirt on the back of lorries. Louis Saha wrote it on his boots, Dennis Wise wore the slogan on his t-shirt, and a Preston fan ran onto the pitch with 'Save Chip' written on his bare back. There were 'Save Chip' banners everywhere: at football, cricket, rugby, darts, indoor bowls, concerts, even WWF in America. We even heard of people being searched before they went on the sports discussion programme *On Side* with John Inverdale to make sure they didn't have banners to hold up during filming, but my personal favourite was when there was one held up behind Tony Blair while he was making a speech.

Everyone latched on to it. At one stage I even had a chat with a PR company who said we spend years and millions of pounds trying to do viral campaigns and yet yours has blown everything out of the water. Then they suggested putting three stripes on the banners and making 'Save Chip' into an Adidas brand. But *Soccer AM* was never about selling out.

Suddenly, Chip had had celebrity thrust upon him and all the tabloids were running stories on the phenomenon and were trying to track him down. It got to the point where Chip actually called the news desk of one of the papers and asked them whether it was worth any money if he could tell them that he knew who Chip was. When the paper said yes, Chip called me and asked me if I would mind if he revealed who he was. 'Of course I bloody do,' I said. 'It's not about you it is about what you stand for.' Thankfully, he's a top bloke and he decided against it.

Sarah was understandably getting moody with the 'Don't Let

Sarah Win!' bit of the campaign, as she was being made out as an evil bully who was controlling Chip. People often ask me what happened to Chip. The answer is I'm still in touch with him and that he not only married Sarah but they have also had a baby girl called Poppy who's a Coventry fan, like Chip. Sadly this has made his rationing even scarcer. Chip now has this strange existence where whenever people discover that he's called 'Chip' and he knows me, they put two and two together and suddenly he gets treated like royalty, because he is Chip, *the* Chip.

The campaign is still running and every so often a 'Save Chip' banner will glimmer in a football crowd somewhere.

THE **REAL** CHIP

I thought it was about time we revealed the man behind the legend of the save chip campaign. He is actually called Paul Gardener, he's from Stratford and he supports Cov.

Even though the campaign wasn't about him in the end and was about the average man/woman being denied the right to watch football, I've asked him to write a few words about what it was like to be Chip.

'I've been a "Chip" since I was 12, a nickname inherited from my dad. It stuck through the years without much comment by new friends and colleagues. My younger brother became "Micro-Chip."

Then Lovebucket hit on something that raised the profile of his show, involving my soon-to-be Mrs — Sarah. The fact that she wouldn't let me watch football all day, everyday, Tim thought unreasonable and the "Save Chip" campaign was launched.

People I had known for years would ask, "Are you the Chip, the one that needs saving?" Girls would phone their boyfriends asking them to guess who they were with. Blokes would laugh, mock, feel sorry for me. Journeys up the motorway now involved spotting "SAVE CHIP" stickers and writings in the muck on the back of lorries.

*In my eyes this was a misplaced "crusade" which grew and the campaign started appearing in newspapers, the Express ran a headline "Who the *!@# is Chip?" Suddenly we had visions of a potential money spinner by revealing my identity. There could have been cash, and maybe a photo-shoot with Sarah in a pinny and rolling pin stood behind me, and me in my Cov strip looking the beaten man.*

Luckily Tim saw sense one day and the campaign slowly came to an end. I managed to hold on to my wife and marriage. Occasionally I'll see SAVE CHIP mugs, stickers and graffiti but what is a real laugh is when new friends and colleagues find out who I "was" and the drinks are bought and I'm now called a "legend!"'

As a postscript to this, if you don't want to get yourself into a position like Chip, where he's controlled by Sarah, I have a great idea. Simply create a book of seven tokens which she can cash in at any time to make you do things you don't want to do. And the rest of the time, she has to leave you alone. When she cashes them in, you have to do whatever she wants you to do. Spend time with her friends, go shopping, have dinner parties, et cetera. It's the greatest present you can give your long-suffering other half, who puts up with you permanently watching sport. However, make sure you can include some small print that says the tokens can't be used during big football occasions like derbies or Cup finals.

RIDICULOUS THEORIES

As I've said before, there are some fans who love their facts and figures, which is why on *Soccer AM* I used to love winding people up. We once carried a story on *Soccer AM* that FIFA had discovered that because of a variety of factors like subsidence and climate change, many of the world's goalposts had shrunk into the ground and that the difference in height between a set of posts at one end of a ground and the set at the other could be as much as three inches. That's nearly half a ball's difference. We then mentioned that in a survey of Premiership clubs, Everton was found to have the lowest crossbar in the country, which, in turn, would explain why they had hit the crossbar the most times, a fact we had checked with the Opta Index. Then we flashed up a picture of the goal at the Park End and deliberately called it the Gwladys Street End just for the hell of it.

That week, we had more emails and letters from irate Everton fans moaning we had mixed up the ends of the ground than we did from anyone questioning the validity of the story itself, ludicrous though it was. Of course we never owned up to it. We just put it out there and let people believe what they want.

The trouble is that once you start that kind of thing you can't really help yourself. We also featured a spoof story about this revolutionary new gel called 'Oxy Boot Gel' that the top Premiership players were using to make their boots stickier, the theory being that if their boots were tacky they would have better close control. Then we'd show pictures of players rubbing this gel on their shirts so they could take some out on to the pitch with them, when what they were really doing is just rubbing Vicks into their chests like Patrick Vieira used to do back then. Bizarrely, a few years later, we had someone who came to work on the show called John Dyson (he's the 'Yorkshire News' reader) who had fallen for it hook, line and sinker. He was gutted when we told him it wasn't true because he'd told all his mates about it.

Soon, though, we found ourselves putting in deliberate mistakes all over the place, just to amuse ourselves and to wind people up, like calling Walsall 'Warsaw' all the time or calling Bayern Munich, 'Bryan Munich', and we used to call Borussia Mönchengladbach 'Borussia Monchenflapjack'. Sure enough, the letters flooded in to such an extent that I started a new item called 'Gone Fishing' whereby I would deliberately make a mistake, wait for all the emails to come pouring in and then reveal the names of the people I'd reeled in.

What it did make me realise was that one thing you can never do in football is get your facts and figures wrong. You can say or do what you like but God help you if you get the name of a stand wrong…

KICKING A BALL THROUGH A HOLE

If you've ever watched *Soccer AM* you will have seen the game we always played at the end of the show in the car park. Basically, it was a group of blokes in a car park, kicking a ball through a hole. We had 'ChiPs', 'LobStar', 'Feed The Goat (And He Will Score)', 'Feed Sven' and, more recently, 'the Road To Wembley'. It's amazing how much enjoyment you can get from watching some people trying to kick a ball through a hole.

I think my personal favourite, though, has to be the Eastern European substitutes in 'Feed The Iron Curtain'. We used to watch all this old footage of European football and the subs were always the same when they were warming up. Basically, they would just run up and down the touchline half a dozen times, do a few star jumps and then go on. This has always made me think – were there more muscle tears and hamstring strains back then? Maybe the modern warm-up routines are just mumbo-jumbo. I mean, I've never seen my cat warm up before chasing birds round the garden, and she's never pulled a hamstring. Do we really need to do it? Anyway, I digress. So we decided to recreate them in 'Feed The Iron Curtain' with Fenners and Sheephead wearing red CCCP tracksuits and blond wigs and just warming up throughout the entire game.

The greatest moment of 'Feed The Iron Curtain' came when Frank McAvennie had a go. When he took his shot, he missed but the ball rebounded back to him and he just smacked it again out of frustration only this time it went straight into Fenners' face, knocking him over. It was so good we named the car park after him. McAvennie that is, not Fenners. The great thing about kicking-the-ball-through-the-hole games, is they now seem to be on every pitch at half-time. I'm not saying we were the first to ever do it, but we certainly made it popular. People are now kicking balls through holes in big cardboard pies, sheds, backs of cars, the list is endless, but always makes for a good laugh.

THE BOUNCE**BACK**ABILITY CAMPAIGN

Getting the word 'bouncebackability' into the dictionary was one of the highlights of my time at *Soccer AM*. It all began when Iain Dowie said the word 'bouncebackability' in a post-match press-conference. Neil Smythe, who's the producer of *Soccer AM* and the intelligent one, came into the ideas meeting the next day and said, 'I think you'll find Iain Dowie is like William Shakespeare – he's made up a new word for the English language. I've never heard it and it's not in the dictionary.' But Neil being the big square he was thought it would be a great idea to see if we could get it in the dictionary.

So we rang up the Collins English Dictionary and asked them how we get a new word into the dictionary and they said once it is in common use it would be included. So we set about trying to encourage everybody we knew to use it and before we knew it, everyone from players in post-match interviews to politicians in Parliament were using it. It was on the radio, television, on the internet, everywhere. You name it, people were saying 'bouncebackability'.

On reflection, it was just a bit of fun but it really seemed to register with people and the whole campaign just snowballed. Eventually, we got a call off Collins to say that it was going in, and the good news is, you still hear it in interviews to this day. But only by managers whose teams are in trouble.

---

bouncebackability **n.** *informal* (especially in sport) the capacity to recover quickly from a set back: *promotion chasing sides need to show the requisite bouncebackability after defeat*.

THE SVEN WAXWORK

One of the things in hindsight I'm astonished we did was try and get a waxwork of Sven-Goran Eriksson made. It seems like he's been such an enemy to England fans and the press for a long time now. But there was a time not so long ago when me, you and everyone else in the country seemed to love having Sven-Goran Eriksson as our national coach. England were unbeaten, we were playing attractive football (5–1 away in Germany!?!?) and for once it looked like we were finally about to fulfil our potential on the international stage. On *Soccer AM* we even dedicated our end game, Ball Through the Hole, to him. We had a giant caricature of his head and the idea was to kick the ball into his mouth. So given that this was the closest we had ever been to the Second Coming of the Lord I decided to start a petition to get a waxwork of Sven made by Madame Tussauds.

So I called Madame Tussauds and asked how we would go about getting a model made of a celebrity. They told me that if we could prove there was sufficient public demand for a waxwork they would consider it so I put this on the show and as always with *Soccer AM* campaigns the demand was so high they set up a separate email address for anyboy wanting to support our new appeal to have Sven cloned. In wax.

Eventually, the response was such that they decided to go ahead and create a Sven waxwork as part of an England themed exhibition, with David Beckham and the rest of the team also included. Job done, or so we thought. But when we asked Madame Tussauds if we could have first dibs on it as a feature for *Soccer AM*, they said no, because it wasn't our idea. That was bad enough but then they said that it had actually all been the Football Association's idea. So I asked the woman at Tussauds again. 'So you are telling me I am lying and we weren't the first people to put that idea to you?' I said to her.

'No I'm not saying you're lying,' she insisted, 'But it was the FA's idea.' It was as if the FA had hijacked the whole concept and she had been told to go along with it. I was furious. I didn't hate Sven as our national manager, and I'm sure that he'll do well at Man City. But after his disappointing exit as England coach, I always wonder what happened to that waxwork, and where it is now.

Out of all the things I've given to the game, this was by far the most pointless.

BODY**BUILDING** FOR THE **COMMON** MAN

Seeing footballers doing goal celebrations inspired from stuff they've watched on *Soccer AM* always made me proud. Direct influence to what was going on on a football pitch: that was something I could have only ever dreamed about. For example, there was the Eastern European sub warm-up, there was my version of hip-hop dancing I was famed for doing on the show, and more recently, there was the bodybuilding, muscle-man pose. Getting players to do that has to be one of my favourite achievements as I've always been fascinated by bodybuilders. From day one on *Soccer AM*, I'd often started posing for the cameras, claiming I had zero percent body fat and I was 'cut'. Fenners and the boys in the crew used to shout lines from Arnold Schwarzenegger's classic documentary *Pumping Iron*, the most famous being 'You're not ready' and 'Show them the whole thing!' Ten years later, when I was thinking about ideas for a new t-shirt giveaway I thought that a t-shirt with 'Show them the whole thing!' being showcased by a Fan of the Week posing down would make good telly. It was only a matter of weeks before the whole nation was sending pictures of themselves in.

While we fully expected the really fit guys to contribute, we were taken aback by the number of blokes with awful guts and man boobs who sent their pictures in. Say what you like, but I defy anyone to look at a film of a fat, hairy, middle aged man in tiny briefs thinking he's Mr Universe and not laugh. But , as I say, what was always more satisfying from my point of view, was when it made its way onto football pitches, with players showing the 'Whole Thing' as a goal celebration.

EASY, EASY!

Influencing players on the pitch to do celebrations was one thing; but to actually influence the fans into chanting 'Easy, Easy!' when their team scored was pure ecstasy. This came about from writing a random sketch where two masked wrestlers would have a fight in everyday locations such as shopping centres, public swimming pools and so on. The winning wrestler, which was always the red one, and played by Fenners, would chant, 'Easy, Easy!' which was stolen from Big Daddy back in the Seventies. It wasn't long before fans were using it to mock the oppo fans after they'd scored. My proudest moment was after Chelsea won the League away at Bolton, John Terry, Frank Lampard and co did the 'Easy!' chant with the Chelsea fans.

THE STAR ON THE ENGLAND SHIRT

I think the most important thing we did at *Soccer AM* whilst I was there was get the star on the England shirt. If you look at the shirts of all of the international teams that have won the World Cup you'll notice that they all feature one gold star for each time they have won the competition. All of the teams, that was, except England. So when we received a letter at *Soccer AM* from a viewer pointing this out we decided to do something about it.

When we wrote to the Football Association asking why we didn't have a star we were told that the famous Three Lions that we have on the shirt are actually more important than having a gold star. It struck me as being a slightly arrogant stance and one that needed challenging. After all, every other country that's won the World Cup celebrates it by putting a star on the national team's shirt so why shouldn't we? It was time for another campaign. So we badgered the FA and got everybody to write to them and eventually they gave in. Credit where credit's due, because initially their attitude was 'we're not doing it'. But because of the response to the campaign, they decided to introduce a gold star to the new England shirt. They even sent me a plaque in recognition of the campaign. Too many people criticise the FA for being old-fashioned and never looking forward but I had nothing but admiration for them for doing that. My only regret is that I can't remember the name of the viewer who was responsible for pointing out the lack of the star. It was his idea and we got all the credit for it.

THE FANS OF THE WEEK

As you know by now, I'm against fundamentalist football fans, so-called 'real fans', who are supposed to be the heart and soul of football. This is completely the opposite to the reality. This was the thinking behind the 'Fans of the Week'. We learnt very early on at

Soccer AM that we should never feature 'real fans' on the show, primarily because 'real fans' tend to be the most boring people on the planet. Try to see it from my position as a producer. If you've got a guy who says he goes home and away and hasn't missed a match for 35 years, he's not going to be that entertaining, is he? As footballers would say, no disrespect to them but we used to have fans of the week that we got from the local supporters club and we would just end up with seven of the dullest people imaginable. These were blokes who were more interested in the politics of the boardroom than what was happening on the pitch. They had no social life, no outside interests, no friends. They just weren't normal. Normal people do other stuff. Normal people ring up and tell their friends they can't go to the match because they're too hungover. Don't normal people play football themselves too? So we steered clear of 'real fans' because in my eyes true football fans are people who go to matches when they want to, who have freedom of choice and whose life is not controlled by a fixture list, but by their minds.

SHOWBOATING

I may stand corrected, but I believe I first used the phrase 'showboating' in a footballing context on TV. Me and my mates had used it for everything from darts to pool and I just thought that we could use it in the show, even though it originated from boxing. I remember one day going round the Sky office asking everybody, 'If I said showboating what would that mean to you?' And they would reply, 'I suppose it means skilful.' From that day on, we began using the word showboating on *Soccer AM*.

The first showboat we ever featured was Gianfranco Zola, a hero of mine, who somehow had crossed the ball with his right leg behind his left leg. It was the first time any of us had seen that done and it had left us all speechless. When it started we would struggle to find enough material to fill the slot each week. It seemed to be the nature of the game in the 1980s and 1990s that displaying skill was frowned upon. Managers, it seemed, just didn't want the fancy-dans or the crowd pleasers. They wanted battlers, cloggers and workhorses. It's indicative of the way the game has changed that by the time I left *Soccer AM* we were spoilt for choice when it came to choosing our showboating moments. Even the word has become part of football lingo. Nowadays, if a player can do a lovely bit of skill they will and they'll be lauded for it. By far the greatest achievement on *Soccer AM* was to feature skills like this every week. So much attention on the game is negative, I felt it was really important to get everyone focussing on the great and wonderful side of football.

THE NUTMEG FILES AND TAXI

The flip-side to the great skills of Showboating, were highlighting player's clumsy mistakes and the ultimate humiliation of being nutmegged. Whilst we often had skilful players like Lee Trundle, who played for Swansea, phoning us up and saying, look out for my showboat, with these two categories, it would be teammates on the phone to us, grassing up their mate in true dressing-room banter style. I know players dreaded making it into either of these categories but I'd like to think they saw the funny side of it. If they didn't, so what, we all find it funny when a player on £100,000 a week does an air-shot with an open goal in front of him.

THE CREW

I remember as a kid being on the terraces at Vicarage Road and hearing people shout Lenny Henry's catchphrase from *Tiswas*, 'Oooooooh-kaaaaaaay!' Many years later I like to think *Soccer AM* was the show that put the catchphrases in the stands. If you look on Google, you can find hundreds of catchphrases from the show, all of which were written by me and my merry men. In fact, my greatest achievement as a producer was discovering the on-screen talent of my production crew. People often ask me if the boys who worked on the show were professional actors. The answer is, no, they were just the crew who worked on the show. The first one I discovered was John Fendley, better known as Fenners, who truly is a remarkable talent. He was doing work experience at Sky Sports and I thought he had a good haircut so I asked him if he wanted a job. Little did I know what a great character actor he was. From Barry to Stan Hibbert, the guy is just class. Also, for comedy value we'd exaggerate the personalities of all the crew members who were featured on the show. And they've made lots of people laugh up and down the years. I got Joe, who was nicknamed Sheephead because of his wool-like hair, to take his shirt off one week for a one-off gag which I was calling Topless Weather. The gag being that it was a man who was topless, not a woman. I know, not that funny, but he turned it into a brilliant slot which lasted five years, and still when he's walking around streets people come up asking what the weather's like. Tubes started out as the Test Tube Baby where we dressed him up in just a towel to look like a nappy, and he ran around like a loony.

But at the start of one season I realise we hadn't used him much the season before so I hatched a plan that he would ask the guests one question, and one question only. Again, I thought it would last about a week. He ended up going to premieres and interviewing Hollywood movie stars, but with only one question. Neil and Robbie will be most famed for their roles as Colonel and Ginger. Colonel who was up-tight and liked to drink, Ginger who had wooden legs and only said 'Draa, draa!' Their job every week was to come out and take the mickey out of celebrities. It was like shooting fish in a barrel. Rocket was the youngest member of the team, who'd started working with us when he was fifteen years old every Saturday. He was always the butt of short-people jokes. And I can't write a book without mentioning other important people on the show: John Dyson, Aldo, Ian Mennear, Luke O'Reilly, Chris Nutbeam, Doctor Chee, Dan Gordon and Geoff the Ref. Sorry for all those I've missed out but there are hundreds of you and my memory is going.

Whilst I was working at the Big Breakfast I tried my hardest to talk to people about football, but there were only three people who would oblige: Chip, who is an important man and head of film research now, but worked there as a runner, looked after the chickens at the house and is a Cov fan; Simon Howley, who was better known as Barnsley because he came from, of course, Barnsley; and Andy Harris, a life-long Arsenal fan.

When I got the job of producing *Soccer AM* I thought I better get some help and phoned Andy as I knew he was looking for a job and was a good producer. Without Andy the show would never have been the success it was. He is as tenacious and persuasive as they come and made *Soccer AM* feel a lot bigger than it was. He was better known to the *Soccer AM* viewers as 'Shandy – the Gooner in the Gallery'. You may also know him as one of the finest Pat Butcher and Mike Reid impersonators in the world. Sadly Andy died recently, leaving his wife and his two boys, who are committed Gooners. I will dearly miss his football banter. He was a great friend.

THANK YOU AND **GOODBYE**

When I announced I was leaving *Soccer AM* it came as a bit of shock to many people but it had been coming. I had been on the programme for well over 10 years and it was high time for me to try something new. In that decade, I had taken a tiny show and with the help of a lot of talented, extremely dedicated people and Rocket, turned it into one of the most talked about and most respected programmes on television. I had worked ridiculously long hours, writing, producing and presenting it; I had given up my weekends and my family life to do it and now, I figured, it was time for a change. I think a lot of the success of the show was down to my bosses, Mark Sharman, who initially gave me the job, and then Vic Wakeling, the big boss, who had the confidence in me to let me experiment and make mistakes. They gave me the freedom to develop the show, which not many producers are lucky enough to get.

A couple of days after my contract ran out, I received a letter from Sky, informing me that my free Sky subscription would now be turned off as I was no longer an employee of the company. Some people get a carriage clock or some flowers when they leave a job they've been in for ages. Loyal football players get a testimonial. I got my Sky cancelled. Ha ha.

The earliest picture of me with a football.
With my brother James.

My mother sewed a Chelsea badge
on a tracksuit and told me it was official
merchandise. In those days this was the
closest you could get.

My first taste of silverware playing for Christchurch primary school. I had the footballer pose,
on one knee, down to a tee.

Tasting more victory at my secondary school in a five-a-side tournament.

Me sporting my Chelsea replica shirt, half-time in Andy Dibbs's garden during the Everton-Man Utd 1985 FA Cup Final.

My brother
James and Ginger.

My brother's
obituary in
the Watford
programme.

My brother's obituary in the Watford programme.

Me in a village
in Vietnam,
just before my
mountain hell.

This was my cub representative team. I was proud to get in the team, but sadly I had to wear a Leeds shirt.

Tacchini ski jacket, bleached jeans from the knees down, covered in jewellery, I was King of the Casuals.

Holidaying in the 80s: I promise you, Speedos were cool back then

School days and the Gary Shaw wedge. The best haircut in Hertfordshire.

Soccer AM and the worst haircut in Hertfordshire.

Barry Proudfoot: The best character I ever invented. Fenners really brought him to life.

You've guessed it…
Bono and The Edge.

Robbie as Fixtures Man, with his
catchphrase, 'Like theeeese!'

Colonel and Ginger,
'Draaa, draaa!'

We won more awards than *The Lord of the Rings*.

The England Star. One of our great
achievements on *Soccer AM*.

Liverpool fans questioning
my sexuality.

My beloved signed Joey Jones shirt, which is my prized possession. It's a Chelsea second kit from back in the Eighties, the only one we had coloured jade.

Rushie and me playing at a tsunami charity match. In my mind I won this ball.

The hardest thing about leaving *Soccer AM* is the thought that I might no longer be influencing the game I love so much. I won't be giving anything back. I won't be continuing my struggle to show the positives of the game and keep negativity at the door. However, you can't keep a good man down, so no doubt I'll see you on TV doing football shows very soon.

PS After modelling *Soccer AM* on the FA Cup Final build-up shows, one of my proudest moments had to be when I actually became a part of the FA Cup Final day by taking the official match ball from the studios in London to Cardiff in a helicopter for the Liverpool-Arsenal clash. I did it with David James as my special guest. In true *Soccer AM* fashion, there was a twist. All I had to do was take the shiny new match-day ball to the stadium, but in my stupidity I left the ball with Bradley Walsh and Jason McAteer for a couple of minutes, and while my back was turned they both decided to draw their initials on it. At the beginning of the match, as directors always do, they had a close-up of the ball at kick-off, and you could clearly see 'BW' and 'JM' scrawled onto it. I have to say I think this was brilliant – can you imagine Jason and Bradley just sitting there, wetting themselves. No better than a couple of kids.

5
LOVEJOY'S
LEGENDS

Legends of the game are normally thought of as being Pele, Maradona, Cryuff, Bobby Charlton, Beckenbauer etc. This is undoubtedly true, but I've never met any of them. As everyone who loves football knows, sometimes your legends are not the obvious ones. Everyone's legends are individual to themselves. Some people will have you believe that there's a magic list somewhere of genuine legends at each club. There are Man Utd fans who like Jesper Olsen above George Best. There are probably some Scousers who prefer Sammy Lee above Kenny Dalglish. And there is nothing wrong with this. I've got hundreds and legends and heroes from the game but I've decided to pick a few that I've had the good fortune to meet and have really impressed me. Oh, and I've also put Mickey Thomas in this list as well.

I do get starstruck though. When I meet players from the present era I'm fine but when I encounter the players I idolised when I was growing up it's an entirely different story. Take Ray Wilkins. He used to work at Sky quite a bit and whenever he saw me in the studio he would always say 'Alright Chelsea Boy!' and I would just go bright red. It was pathetic. Mind you, it was the same with Kenny Dalglish when I met him. I was like a big kid. I played in a match with his son Paul once with my team the Badgers and not played very well. Then I got the chance to play in a charity match for the Badgers for the tsunami appeal. I'd never met Kenny before and as we were going out onto the pitch he came over to me and said 'Hello Tim, how are you?' Then he smiled and said 'I've heard you've suffered a dip in form recently?' For him to say that to me was just hysterical.

Thinking about it, it has been the same with Kevin Keegan, Glenn Hoddle and pretty much any of the players who were famous when I was young. Put me in front of any movie star or pop star and it doesn't faze me. Put me in front of Butch Wilkins though and I'm gone.

When you actually play football with some of these legendary names you soon realise just why they made it in the professional game and you didn't. They may have lost a yard and put a few pounds on but they can still run rings round most ordinary players and they all seem to have this innate desire, this appetite for the game that never fades. I once played at the old Wembley on the same side as Ian Rush and Peter Beardsley. Anyway, I was desperately trying to score and when Beardsley set off on one of his mazy runs he hit this ball across the area and I sensed my chance. As the ball was coming over, though, Rushie shouted over to me, 'You've gone too soon Tim!' and sure enough I missed the ball and it ran through to Rushie who stuck it in at the back post. That's why he's a legend. He knows exactly where and when to run whereas I'm just this eager beaver haring towards the goal at breakneck speed.

Micky Hazard is another example. Even now he's still one of the most skilful players I have ever seen in my life. I played with him a few years ago at a five-a-side tournament. He took me to one side as we were warming up. 'Come here Tim,' he said, 'I've learnt this new trick.' He had me defending against him, and he kicked the ball with his heel and then quickly flicked it with his toe on the same foot in a split second. It was majestic. He then insisted I try it. I said, 'Mickey, I've learnt all the tricks I want to learn. I'm too old now.' Mickey said, 'You're never too old to learn new tricks.' That's the difference. He's still up for trying new things even though he retired some years ago.

Liverpool and Chelsea legend Joey Jones is my favourite though. I played with him for Rhyll against *Hollyoaks* in a charity match once, when someone from the *Hollyoaks* team went over the ball and caught me. So as I was there squaring up to this bloke, Mickey Thomas came over. 'Don't worry, Tim,' he whispered, 'Joey will get him.' Sure enough, the next time this fella got the ball, Joey went straight through him and took him out completely. It was incredible. I've never seen anyone with such determination to win the ball. Every tackle, every header, Joey was there, his desire to win the ball was amazing. Complete and absolute dedication. Win at all costs. And it was only a charity game.

Here, then, are some of my other legends…

Mickey Thomas

Mickey Thomas is my all-time favourite. I always remember him from the time on *Match of the Day* when he dived after a tackle was made on him and then he just got up and winked at the camera. That's Mickey, a genuine showman. The great thing about Mickey is that even today he still loves playing football and that's always been the way with him, regardless of what financial situation he's been in or whatever crisis he's in the middle of. A lot of players from his era have become bitter and twisted because they've missed out on the big money the players get today, but not Mickey. I asked him about that once and he said 'Tim, I have had the chance to play football at the highest level for Manchester United, Chelsea and Wales and whatever happens to me, nobody can ever take that away from me.'

I feel very privileged to have Mickey Thomas as a friend, and I often used him on *Soccer AM*, when he always entertained us. He's always got a good joke and a great story, and he genuinely is one of life's good guys. But saying that, he did spend a bit of time at Her Majesty's Pleasure for dealing in dodgy currency. We always used to take the mickey out of Mickey, pardon the pun, and he always took it in great spirit. We even went as far as making up Mickey Thomas fake £50 notes. Going from watching him from the terraces to counting him as a friend has been one of the great benefits of my career.

Frank Worthington

I love Frank Worthington, a true showman. Every time he used to come on *Soccer AM* he used to do the same gag every time without fail. 'I'm doing a lot of after-dinner speaking at the moment,' he'd say. 'Last night, I did the Dwarves Convention . . . got a standing ovation . . . didn't know anything about it.' Before he came on we used to sit in the office wondering just when he'd do the dwarf gag again and sure enough he never let us down. I love him for that. I never saw his after-dinner speech, but I understand he was the best: entertainer on the pitch, and a definite entertainer in real life.

I once took my team The Badgers to play against an Old Boys XI in Spain. Looking back, they had a hell of a side. Jimmy Case was playing, Emlyn Hughes, Phil Thompson. Emlyn was magnificent. He played the game wearing a bin liner under his shirt, because the old school view was if you played in a bin liner you would lose weight. There we were in Spain in blazing 80-degree plus heat and there was Crazy Horse in a bin liner. Amazing. But it was Frank Worthington who was the main attraction. We flew in on the day of the game, played the match (and won I have to add) and then got so horrifically drunk that we all ended up in the pool at the hotel. We also lost the trophy we'd won too. Where's Pickles when you need him, eh?

The next morning we dragged ourselves down to breakfast, conscious that we were pushed for time to get our flight back. As we were leaving, though, we noticed Frank lying by the pool in speedos and sunglasses with his hair gelled back. As we gathered all our bags in the hotel foyer I went over to Frank to remind him that he'd better get a move on if he was going to catch the flight home. He just turned his head, lifted his sunglasses, told me not to worry and then carried on sunbathing. Now that's class.

Robbie Savage

If I was a footballer I'd definitely want to be Robbie Savage. Why? Because he's hated by everyone – apart from his own team's fans – and that, in my opinion, is a massive compliment to him as a footballer. Everywhere you go people say, 'I don't like Robbie Savage' but the truth is that they don't like Robbie Savage the player, not the man.

The real Robbie Savage is a genuinely nice bloke and every time he's been on *Soccer AM* he has always been an absolute gentleman. He's a great laugh too. We used him for so much material on the show because for some reason he always seemed to get hit on the head; the referee Paul Durkin (or 'Paul Gherkin' as we called him) even punched him by accident when signalling which way a free-kick should go. Often, he would send in video clips from his mobile phone of him doing impressions of other players and insist that we use it in on the programme. And of course, we would oblige.

Ultimately, I just think Robbie plays football the right way. Yes, he enjoys himself, yes he gets stuck in and yes he winds up all the other players but that's because he is an intense man. I tell you what, though, if you had 11 Robbie Savages in your team you wouldn't be far off winning the title.

Jimmy Bullard

My favourite modern player, you may be surprised to hear, isn't a Chelsea player. It's Fulham's Jimmy Bullard. Everything that man does is class and any young players looking to get on in football should take a look at how he conducts himself and how he plays the game. Just complete, absolute dedication. What people don't know is that he's the same in whatever he decides to do. He's a scratch golfer, for example, and he's also a top fisherman too and has won countless competitions. It's for things like this and the fact that he did one of the most ridiculous leapfrog-cum-dives in a goalmouth melee against Arsenal that we re-named the *Soccer AM* studio doors as the 'Jimmy Bullard's Back Door'. It was the least we could do. As a player he's that box-to-box, one hundred and ten per cent cliché but he does it all with a smile on his face. It's just brilliant seeing a pro thoroughly enjoying his career. So many of them look back and think 'I wish I had more fun when I was playing'. Jimmy won't have those regrets.

Gerry Armstrong

Aside from being one of the greatest players Northern Ireland's ever had, Gerry Armstrong is also the unsung hero of Sky Sports because he is the oracle of world football. Believe me, he knows everything about every single football team in the world. If I ever need to know anything about any football topic I don't Google it, I Gerry Armstong it. His knowledge is unbelievable. He can do Spanish football, German football, he can do Dutch football, French football, African football, Russian football. I bet if you pressed him, he could probably tell you something about the qualifying rounds in the Ecuador League Cup. I have no idea how he managed to keep his marriage intact because he must spend the whole of his life watching football and doing precious little else.

John Terry

I think JT was probably born a legend. I remember when I used to go to games and watch the teams warm up on the pitch before the kick-off and while all the foreign players would be wearing tracksuit, hats and gloves, JT would be out there warming up in shorts and a t-shirt. And this was in the middle of winter. I asked him once why he only came out in shorts and t-shirts and he just said, 'Because it feels good.'

The other thing about JT is that he is genuinely as hard as nails. If he goes down and stays down, you know he is injured. As everyone saw in the Carling Cup Final in 2007 when he got knocked unconscious, he will put his head in when everybody else is letting it go. People were surprised when he discharged himself from hospital a couple of hours later to return to the after-match get-together. I wasn't.

John Terry is like a player from a different era. He has this never-say-die spirit and a bravery that goes way beyond the call of duty. And yet he is remarkably composed when he is playing. Rarely does he get involved in any handbags and if someone does decide to have a tear up with him, he'll walk away safe in the knowledge that he's already the hardest man out there.

We had some great footage of JT on *Soccer AM* when he was training with Chelsea once and it demonstrated just how much he loves playing the game. As the players were having a kickabout, JT got the ball and was about to be tackled by Marcel Desailly when he nutmegged him. He then ran around squealing like a small child. He was so excited that he'd nutmegged one of his team-mates that he just couldn't contain himself.

But that's JT for you. You can tell that every day he goes to the training ground he absolutely loves being there and that even if he wasn't a professional he'd still be playing in a Sunday league team somewhere. And that's what Chelsea fans love about him. He gives you this cast iron guarantee that whenever he walks on the pitch he will give you everything he's got.

Robbie Fowler

What makes Robbie a legend is not his football, which everyone knows is God-like, but that he is very much his own man. That's what sets him apart from many footballers and why he came on the show – because he wanted to, not because he had to. He's clever too. So clever, in fact, that he has a property portfolio so large that I've heard he actually owns Oldham. He also has a very special place in the history of *Soccer AM*. He was the first really high-profile player to appear on the show and the first to appear three times, thereby claiming the *Soccer AM* match ball, signed by the crew, which is just ridiculously generous. The fact that he had come on the show opened all kinds of doors for *Soccer AM*. Suddenly, if the show was good enough for Robbie, it was good enough for everybody else.

Robbie also helped change the attitude of *Soccer AM*. His first visit was after Chelsea had beaten Liverpool at Stamford Bridge 4–2 and Chelsea had been down 2–0 at half-time in the Cup. I was having a bit of banter with Robbie and suddenly the moment felt right for me to gently remind Robbie of the final score using my digits – two on one hand, four on the other, whilst saying to him, 'Remember, Robbie, it was 4–2.' Robbie then continued to cane me throughout the rest of the show and I realised that I can have a lot more banter with the footballers than I'd thought possible. Dressing-room humour had arrived in the *Soccer AM* studio.

Neil Ruddock

Neil 'Razor' Ruddock has to be one of the funniest men alive. I imagine having him in your dressing room would have been an asset to your football club. The first time I met Razor was when I was working on the Big Breakfast and I had to do an interview with John Scales. John was injured and all the players were turning up at Anfield about to go on the team bus for an away match. Razor came over and introduced himself. John Scales said, 'Are you fit, Razor?' and Razor replied, 'You know the score, John. If you're as good as me you don't have to be fit.'

Later on, he was a regular guest on *Soccer AM*, told some great stories but always joined in with the show and the fun. The only downside to knowing Razor Ruddock is it hurts. Literally. I would always take the mickey out of Razor before he came on the show and after he'd retired I'd say, 'He's one of our biggest guests, in fact he's as big as a house' and suchlike. The first thing he would do is stroll on and give me a dead leg and Helen a kiss. That's Razor – part hard man, part gentleman.

Carlton Palmer

'Carlton, Hit Les, Demand It' is what we always used to shout at Carlton Palmer. The expression was from the infamous Graham Taylor documentary. Carlton still to this day denies having watched it, which I doubt very much. Carlton has entertained me many a time with great stories, none of which I can repeat in this book, all of which you can probably read elsewhere; the great thing about Carlton is the fact that he's willing to speak his mind. He also backs up his opinions with such confidence, yet often they turn out to be, well, wrong. A good example of this was him telling us all that Sol Campbell's move to Man Utd from Spurs was a 'done deal'. He refused to entertain the idea of Sol going anywhere else. Subsequently, Sol Campbell moved to Arsenal and I never let Carlton live it down.

Carlton is also another one of those great entertainers who didn't mind joining in with the fun on *Soccer AM*. There was a stage when I did magic tricks every week and Carlton kindly volunteered to let me do the guillotine trick and put his neck on the line, quite literally, for entertainment's sake. He will never really know how close he came to losing his head that day – it's only the click of a switch that stops you losing your head, and I was so nervous I nearly forgot to do it.

Luther Blissett

A genuine hero of mine for many reasons. When I went to watch Watford in the Fourth Division, he partnered Ross Jenkins up front and scored a load of goals. He also played for England and Milan but that's not why we named the *Soccer AM* Luther Blissett stand after him. The reason we did this was Watford got Torquay in the Cup one year, and a few of us from *Soccer AM* decided to go down and watch the match with Helen Chamberlain, my co-presenter who's a massive Torquay fan. She was already in the ground and we were picking up tickets from Vicarage Road box office. It was the coldest night there has ever been in the history of Britain, or at least the history of Watford. We were stood outside, freezing cold, when I got a tap on my shoulder, and it was Luther Blissett. I explained the ticket situation to him, and he said, 'Don't worry lads, follow me.' Luther was on the coaching staff at the club at the time, so he led us through this door, down a set of stairs, past the dressing rooms, out of the players' tunnel, onto the pitch, walked us round the outside of the pitch, said hello to a couple of stewards, and we climbed over the wall, into the Torquay fans' area and sat with Helen for free. At that moment we decided we were going to name our stand after Luther Blissett.

One of the funniest moments ever on *Soccer AM* happened with Luther Blissett. There was always this ridiculous story going around that the Milan scouts came and watched Watford play, saw John Barnes, and reported back that they wanted the black player at Watford. When the Milan executives came to buy Barnes, they bought Luther instead. This is the myth, anyway. Luther was obviously aware of this story, and one day on *Soccer AM*, when I talked to him about Milan, I said, 'How did the move come about?' and he replied, 'They wanted John Barnes and they bought me by mistake' and started laughing. It took me by such surprise I laughed along for about five minutes and nearly wet myself. Luther can do no wrong in my eyes.

Chris Kamara

Is there a more enthusiastic person in the game of football than Chris Kamara? He is absolutely irrepressible. When he used to do the previews on *Soccer AM* he would always make a nuisance of himself at the clubs he was visiting. Invariably, he would be under strict instructions from the club as to where he could and couldn't go within the ground and all Chris would do is ignore it and just barge his way into the dressing room anyway and walk up to the players and ask them "Are you fit?" or "Are you leaving then?" It was only because he is so well liked and respected in the game that he could get away with it. The great thing about working with men like Chris was that you saw a different side to them whenever they came on *Soccer AM*. I can't prove it, but to me it seemed like they would much rather be working with us at *Soccer AM* than doing whatever it was they did at Sky Sports.

Paul Gascoigne

Where do you start with someone like Paul Gascoigne? In my view, he is arguably the most talented player that England has ever produced. Sure, Glenn Hoddle, Wayne Rooney and David Beckham may be up there but Gazza in his prime was something else.

Before I left *Soccer AM* I had to compile a DVD and I was looking at the highlights of his career and it was completely breathtaking. Incredible skills, great vision, unbelievable goals. He was a one-off. What really struck me was the sheer enthusiasm he had for the game and the amount of enjoyment he brought to everyone who followed football. If everyone was as cool and calculated in interviews as Alan Shearer and Michael Owen then football would be a poorer place. Hats off to them, they're brilliant players and immaculate professionals, but to have someone like Gazza turn up and do the things he did was such a relief. That he has the talent to back it up, though, was just phenomenal.

Thinking about it, I don't think I've ever met anyone who is as much in love with football as Paul Gascoigne. If you speak to any of the players who played with him, they might have a few things to say about his lifestyle and how things have panned out for him but they'll never openly criticise him. Why? Because all he ever wanted to do was his best for his country and his best at playing football.

Gazza's problem was that he had too much time for everyone. I once had a night out in the West End of London with him and Neil Ruddock after *Soccer AM* one Saturday. As we walked along the street, people were piling out of pubs to see him or coming up to him to get their picture taken with him.

But this was what his life was like, he was such an amazing personality, such a magnet for attention. When I made a documentary with David Beckham, you could see the difference. He has a lot of people around him making sure he has his space. He's the ultimate professional. Paul Gascoigne never had the same luxury. What he does have though is a heart of gold and I would never say a bad word against the man. He is a true entertainer.

What upsets me about Paul Gascoigne is the way our media have treated him. Continually on his case, he's either too fat or too thin, a lot of stories are negative, they just seem to want to destroy him. It's easy to criticise Gazza, but if you weigh it all up, there are many more good things about him than bad. And if you are a tabloid journalist looking for scandal, have another look at the man. At least he's man enough to admit his problems.

On a brighter note, I also love Paul Gascoigne because he scored one of the greatest England goals of all time. I'm referring, of course, to the one he scored against Scotland in Euro 96. I was there behind the goal that day when he scored. It was an exceptional piece of skill. To have the speed of thought and the skill to execute first the flick over Colin Hendry's head and then the volley past Andy Goram was just incredible. What made it more miraculous, as folklore has it, is that in true Gazza style he'd forgotten his boots that day and he was actually wearing a pair of Teddy Sheringham's when he scored. And guess what? They were two sizes too big. Now that's genius.

Charlie Nicholas

I always remember the 'Champagne Charlie' headlines that accompanied the newspaper reports when Charlie Nicholas moved down from Celtic to play for Arsenal. After what had happened to his fellow Scottish poster boy Peter Marinello on his unsuccessful move to Highbury, there was a lot of pressure on Charlie to deliver which I think he did, even though his lifestyle seemed to be of more interest to everyone in the media.

When we finally got the chance to do some work with him on *Soccer Am* it was just fantastic and the fact that he really entered into the spirit of things made it even better. Every time he came on, we'd have screaming girls accompanying his introduction and he'd always wear sunglasses when we were doing an outside broadcast, even it was overcast or throwing it down. It was like he was some kind of rock God, which, looking back, he was really. My favourite thing was when I talked to him abut Scottish football every week and Rangers were dominant in Scotland at the time. It really stuck in his throat and all his compliments were through gritted teeth. But he was a pro. Still is.

Tim Lovejoy

Well, maybe not. But I could have been. We were watching a game of pool on Sky once when the camera closed in on this kid in the stands. He was holding a sign that read: Lovejoy is a Legend. Soon after, I got a letter at *Soccer AM* from the lad in question asking me whether I had seen the sign. So we featured it on the show and me, in my naivety, decided that it was such a good idea that I would send the kid five pounds for his trouble. I also happened to mention that I'd send any other kid that did it five quid if they got seen on TV. Bad move – for me anyway. Within weeks, I was handing out fivers like nobody's business. Kids with 'Lovejoy is a Legend' banners were turning up on Match of the Day, at every sporting occasion, just about anywhere you looked on TV, there was a 'Lovejoy is a Legend' banner. Needless to say, they'd then write in to claim their five pounds. I must have paid out over five hundred quid in the end. Still, it was one of those great marketing things that a lot of people wished they had thought of and proved, yet again, that good hard honest cash can bribe a lot of people.

6

IF YOU'RE GONNA GO

HERE'S WHAT YOU MUST KNOW

I remember the first time I did an interview to publicise *Soccer AM*. I don't want to remember it but it still grates to this day. I had gone in to the interview assuming it was going to be a nice, straightforward piece about the programme and about football, more generally. But it was anything but.

It all started going wrong when the journalist started testing me about my knowledge of Chelsea and I just froze. He kept asking me questions about the FA Cup in 1970 and the Cup Winners Cup in 1971 and I started getting them mixed up. As he fired in another question, I began to get really confused. 'Who scored in the 1971 Cup-Winners' Cup Final?' he said. And I was like 'Do you know what, I don't know.' And I didn't know. I felt like a total spoon.

When the piece came out the journalist had outed me as a fake Chelsea fan. I was distraught. I had travelled all over the country with Chelsea. I had travelled home and away with Chelsea. I had been to every Godforsaken little ground around the country with Chelsea, I had bought scores of Chelsea shirts. I had done the lot, but there I was, outed as a fraud. For a while it really bugged me. I had these panic attacks where I started questioning whether or not I had the right to present a football programme, especially if I wasn't a proper fan. It was like I wasn't worthy any more. It took me a couple of months before I decided that it was actually all a load of rubbish. In the end, I realised that it was no big deal. Why would I give a damn about something that happened when I was two years-old? It was Kerry Dixon and Johnny Bumstead I cared about, not Ossie and Chopper, let alone 1955's hero Roy Bentley.

Besides, what gives anyone the right to question how I enjoy football or how I follow it? From that day on, I simply refused to play the game when I did interviews for the show. Whenever journalists went down the 'You say you're a Chelsea fan but you used to go to Watford' line of questioning I just used to say 'Yep, that's me, the lifelong Watford fan.' Why? Because it was their problem, not mine.

It proved to be a real turning point for me and for *Soccer AM*. There's so much crap said and written about who's the bigger club or who's got the best fans that I just decided to put an end to it there and then. There's nothing to be gained from testing people or catching them out. If somebody doesn't know West Brom's nickname or where Huddersfield play their home games, don't hate them for it. Embrace them.

However, if you are a fan and you do want to go to football matches, here's what I know.

CHOOSE
YOUR SEAT CAREFULLY

Going to a match can be an assault on your senses. In fact, one of my earliest football memories was the odour of fried onions coming from the scores of hot dog stands outside Fulham Broadway tube station. Well, that and the s∗∗∗ from the police horses.

Once you were inside the ground, it seemed as though everybody in there, well in The Shed at least, spent the entire game smoking. Benson and Hedges, Rothmans – there was always that unmistakeable smell of cheap cigarettes. If you didn't smoke, it was hell. Invariably, I would end standing next to some bloke who would miss most of the game because he was too busy rolling his own fags from a little tin.

Exposure to body odour was also a permanent problem in the terraces, made all the worse because it was this tightly packed confined space with no clear escape route. There were times when people never made it to the toilets in time too. Personal hygiene, it seems, never ranked very highly on the football fan's match day checklist.

When the Taylor Report brought about all-seater stadia, I thought that might be the end of the close encounters of the turd kind. Instead, it brought about a whole new kind of problem. Now when you buy your season ticket you could end up sitting next to someone you don't know and/or like not just for 90 minutes but for an entire season. A friend of mine at Stamford Bridge had to sit next to a bloke who would spend the whole game rocking back and forth and just muttering 'Chelsea, Chelsea, Chelsea' all the way through. A month into the season, and my mate just wanted to punch this bloke's lights out. It was driving him insane. He couldn't stand it. Eventually, he confronted the bloke: 'Do you have to do that all the way through the match?' he said. The guy turned to him and just said: 'I don't know what I'm doing.' It was like some pitiful plea for help. In such a situation the only thing you can do is ask the club ticket office to move you to another seat. Now that's fine if you're a season ticket holder at Rochdale or Gillingham and there's plenty of choice on offer but not very likely if there's a ten-year waiting list at Anfield or Old Trafford. In which case you're stuck with the mentalist.

KNOW **YOUR** SILVERWARE

As a football fan you have to know the order of your silverware. When you're challenging for honours on four fronts, like Chelsea, you often find yourself pondering which of the trophies you would rather win at the expense of others. For me, there is a clear pecking order in the importance of the trophies you would want your club to win and, unless you're a modern day Liverpool fan who only cares about the Champions' League, it goes something like this . . .

1   The Premiership

2   The Champions' League

3   The FA Cup

4   The UEFA Cup

5   The Carling Cup

6   The Championship

7   League Two

8   League Three

9   LDV/Johnstone's Paint/Autowindshields/screens (whatever it's called that season)

10 The Rugby World Cup

ESTABLISH A RAPPORT WITH RIVAL FANS

Being a football fan, you have to both know and dislike your rivals. This should be done with friendly banter down the pub, as opposed to beating the living daylights out of each other. In my job I've been privileged enough to attend a lot of great football matches and meet a lot of fantastic footballers. To be honest, though, it is my relationship with the fans that is really special. For whatever reason, it's the Liverpool fans I seem to have the most banter with. Here, after all, is a group of fans that seem to be the only ones in England who can rival continental supporters in their ability to make ridiculous oversized flags. You can imagine my pride, then, when the Kop decided to make one in my honour. The fact that it said 'Lovejoy Sucks Big Fat Cock' for our Carling Cup Final clash is irrelevant.

I can't tell you how happy it made me feel that someone had gone to all that effort, sitting in night after night, making a flag that had my name on it and even though it was insulting it was just the most amazing experience that I had actually got a Liverpool fan somewhere to think, 'Right, I'm going to make a flag which has a pop at Lovejoy'. That fills me with pride.

Remember, these are also the fans that embraced the Middle East culture of taking large framed pictures of their leaders out into the streets, the difference being they carried ones of Rafa Benitez around instead. That was brilliant and just another example of how their obsession for the game is unrivalled.

I recently had a trip up to Anfield with my friend Simon Rimmer, who's the chef off my Sunday morning show *Something for the Weekend*, and a big Liverpool fan. He had promised me director's tickets in the ground. We started by going to a pub and sat with about four generations of Liverpool fans, sporting everything from Bill Shankly ties and Bob Paisley t-shirts to Liverpool FC jewellery. It was great to see the passion that they have for their game. We met Jason McAteer at the game to find out we didn't have director's box tickets. They were nice tickets, but they were in the Liverpool end. I was horrified but the respect they gave me was amazing. When Chelsea went 1–0 down, it felt like half the stand turned and started chanting, 'Lovejoy, Lovejoy, what's the score?' On the outside I was smiling; on the inside I was dying.

And just to continue the banter, can I quickly remind Liverpool fans that they've never won the Premier League and the last time they won the top flight was 18 years ago.

LEARN TO LOATHE RUGBY

If you're going to take being a football fan seriously you have to learn that rugby is the enemy. Rugby is the dark side. I believe it was Helen Chamberlain who was the person who coined the phrase 'egg chasing' to describe rugby and, as usual, she was spot on.

The real reason why no self-respecting football fan should like rugby is because in rugby too much is left to chance. In football, the ball is all-important. If you trying playing with a square ball it just won't work. In rugby the ball is irrelevant. In fact, I've always said you could use a stale loaf of bread to play rugby and still have a half decent game, thereby proving that it is not a game of skill. The way I see it, it's more like a group of thick-set lads playing British Bulldog.

Where I grew up there was a lot of rugby players in the area and there was always banter between the two camps. I don't think that should ever change and I believe that if you are a football fan it is your duty to dislike rugby. You are allowed to like rugby league a bit, but only because it winds rugby union fans up when you tell them that you think it's just a more skilful version of their game.

I confess that I played rugby a couple of times when I was younger but found that it hurt too much. And yes, I'll even watch the occasional game now because I'm friends with a lot of the players like Will Greenwood, Matt Dawson, Lawrence Dallaglio and Austin Healy. They're all really lovely, exceptionally funny blokes and what makes them so easy to get on with is that they are intelligent enough to accept that their game is inferior to football. That said, I do have a lot of respect for anyone who plays rugby because it's a lot of pain for very little gain. Personally, though, my idea of sport isn't one where you get your knees dirty, roll around in the mud for eighty minutes (that's ten less than football), have a little bit of a punch-up and then drink each other's wee in the bar afterwards. You see, that is basically rugby for you. Where with football, it is a game of skill, physique, guile, athleticism, grace, intelligence, entertainment, strategy…

YOU MUST BE SUPERSTITIOUS

There are few species more superstitious than the football fan. Not so long ago, I used to bet on Chelsea with my mates, not down the bookies, the odd 20 quid here and there, but when the results didn't go my way I suddenly began believing that it was my betting that was causing Chelsea to lose. It's nonsense, I know, but bear with me.

It was only when I started betting publicly on *Soccer AM* that it dawned on me that I wasn't the only fan who let superstition get the better of them. I once mentioned on the show that I was so confident of Chelsea beating Barcelona in the Champions League that if we lost I would stand in London's Oxford Street in Barcelona's kit holding a big sign saying 'LOSER'. Needless to say, we lost.

The next season, I had a bet with Liverpool fan James Redmond on the outcome of our Champions' League semi-final. Yet again, Chelsea lost and this time I had to go back to Oxford Street, embarrassing myself in a pink tutu.

What happened next was remarkable. I started getting letters from Chelsea fans saying that it was my fault they were losing these big games because I was betting on them, as if I could actually influence what goes on in the world, like I was Uri Geller or Derren Brown. Often, I would reply, asking the fan whether they thought I was the Son of God? It just baffled me to think that some people thought it was me, and not Jose Mourihno or Frankie Lampard or Stevie Gerrard, that had the most influence on the outcome of the game. And why? Because I happened to have a little bet on it.

Call it straw clutching, barrel scraping or hoping against hope, but I suspect that all fans are superstitious in some way. It's that the strange thought process that says if I wear the same pair of lucky underpants every week when we play then we'll win. But what the hell have underpants got to do with the outcome of a football match? There are too many factors involved in a football match, not least twenty-two players on a pitch with three match officials. Mind you, I would love Jose Mourinho in one of his post-match interviews when he was manager to say: 'For sure, we lost the Premiership title because Tim Lovejoy was not wearing his lucky pants.'

ALWAYS, ALWAYS, ALWAYS HATE THE MOST SUCCESSFUL TEAM

Do the terms ABC or ABU mean anything to you? Well, they should do. As a football fan, it is your duty to hate the most successful team of the moment. In the late 1960s and early 1970s, it was Leeds, or 'Dirty Leeds' to the masses. In the 1980s it was Liverpool. And in the 1990s it was Manchester United. More recently, it has been my team, Chelsea, that has been on the receiving end. Remember, it's not a personal thing. It's just something British football fans need to do . . . and I love them for it. By the way, ABC stands for 'Anyone But Chelsea' and ABU means 'Anyone But United'. . .

MAKE SURE YOU KNOW THE WORDS TO YOUR CLUB'S SONGS

'Carefree where ever you may be,
We are the famous CFC.
And we don't give a f*** whoever you may be,
'Cos we are the famous CFC'

('CAREFREE', SUNG BY CHELSEA FANS TO THE TUNE OF 'THE LORD OF THE DANCE')

I have a friend who has only recently started coming to Stamford Bridge. I have no problem with that. Everyone has to start somewhere so you may as well start at the home of football. He's now got to the point where he is sufficiently confident to start singing at games but let me tell you he really needs to brush up on some of the lyrics.

I caught him in a pub, drunk, having been to Stamford Bridge, banging out what he thought was the words to the song Carefree which is a perennial favourite at the Bridge. As he sang I listened to him and felt compelled to interrupt him. 'What are you singing at the beginning of that song?'

He just shrugged and said, 'Geoffrey wherever you may be . . .'

'Why are you singing that?' I asked him.

'Because that's the words, isn't it?'

'No,' I laughed. 'And where do you get the Geoffrey bit from?'

'Isn't it something to do with Geoff Hurst?' he said.

'Geoff Hurst?'

'Didn't he play for Chelsea or manage them or something?' Somehow, he had made this connection in his mind and just assumed that those were the words. But he's not alone. People get the words wrong in football songs all the time. Ordinarily, that's not a problem when you're just one voice in 40,000 but if you are caught out, it's mortifying. You see, not knowing the words to your club songs is a crime and failing to learn them means you'll always be on the outside looking in when it comes to supporting your club.

When I was a kid I used to take comfort in the fact that we had sung louder than the opposition fans even if we had been hammered. I've no idea why that matters but it does. It's bizarre;

my team's rubbish but we're really loud singers. It's that sense that we're all in this together, that we are the difference, we are the twelfth man.

It's a beautiful thing. The weird thing about the modern day football song is that they all seem to be about the players and not the club. This is a good thing because the songs in the 1980s were often about hooliganism and racism. However, I always think the best songs always have an 'Oi!' in there somewhere. The flip side of this, however, is that players know when they are unpopular because nobody ever sings their name. I would do a list of my top ten favourite football songs but I really can't be arsed. Full marks to Celtic fans though for their Jan Venegoor of Hesselink one, set to the song 'Lily the Pink'. That takes some beating.

I think it must be a proud moment for a football fan to invent a song that gets picked up by your fellow supporters. I made my own stab at lyrical glory once when attempting to set Marcel Desailly's name to the theme tune from the TV Western *Bonanza*. It went something like:

> Dah-da-da-da-da-da-da-Desailly!
>
> Dah-da-da-da-da-da-da-da-da-da-da-da-Oi!

It never caught on.

DON'T BE AFRAID TO DO A U-TURN

As a football fan it is the law for you to hate a certain number of opposition players. Now, before I explain myself I should say that I don't hate these players as people and that I have nothing but the utmost respect for them as players but as a fan it is my duty to hate opposition players. For some reason, though, most of the players I have hated have played for Man Utd. And for some reason, I always do a u-turn and end up loving them.

A classic case in point is Mark Hughes. When he played for Man Utd I thought he was the dirtiest, most hideous player I'd ever seen. He was always leaving his leg in, always slightly late in the tackle, always two-footing centre-halves and always using his elbows. He was a menace. He was an animal. I always thought that the referee should have given him a yellow card before he went on the pitch because it was odds-on he was going to get one anyway and it would just save the ref a job later.

But then he moved to Chelsea, a club I believe he supported as a kid anyway, and as soon as he ran out at Stamford Bridge he became my hero. No longer was he the thug or the hooligan I had hated, now he was just a committed, energetic and aggressive striker who gave his all for the cause. Us fans are so fickle but will never admit it. You'll often hear me saying, 'Yes, I always loved him!'

Another player I've hated then loved is Roy Keane. Full respect to him as a player because he was amazing. But I remember I watched him when he played at Stamford Bridge once and yes, he did all the things I hated but what struck me was that he was never further than ten yards away from the ball throughout the entire match. He was just everywhere. The spirit and the energy he had was just immense. Alex Ferguson owes that man a lot.

Finally, there is David Beckham. When he came down to Chelsea with United I absolutely despised him, I admit it. I thought he was just a corporate showpony and bought into the myth that he cared more about money and modelling than he did about football. But it was on a chance meeting that my opinion changed. I was at the opening of an Adidas store in Oxford Street, London and it was like a Who's Who of Adidas stars. But you couldn't get anywhere near David Beckham. He was the main event. But his manager Terry Byrne came over to me and said that David would like to meet me. People bang on about 'Brand Beckham' all the time and assume he's only interested in making more and more money but nothing could be further from the truth in meeting with him that night.

It was not long after he had moved to Real Madrid and I asked him how he was getting on. He told me that it was a little difficult at the time as the family were living in a rented house, trying to get the kids into school and the paparazzi wouldn't leave them alone 'but as for the football,' he added, 'it is just amazing. I mean, I'm playing with absolute legends in the Bernabeu every week. How good is that?' There was a definite sparkle in his eye when he talked about football and I realised that all my preconceived ideas about him were wrong. There wasn't a single mention of 'Brand Beckham' or about his endorsements. All he was concerned with was his family and his football. And you could tell he loved football.

I went away from that meeting thinking that the world needed to see the real side of David Beckham so I pestered him for six months to agree to do a documentary and all the time he was like, 'nobody wants to see any more of me, everyone's fed up with seeing me on TV.' Eventually, though, I convinced him and we made the documentary and I realised he's the biggest player in the world bar none and his influence on the game has been enormous. People always want to hate him because of his profile but I can promise you that he is just a genuinely nice bloke who happens to be extremely good at football.

DON'T BELIEVE WHAT OTHER FANS TELL YOU

Be careful when you go to football grounds. There's a lot of nonsense spoken, and there are certain myths in football that need to be laid to rest. Perhaps the most infuriating of all though is the idea that everyone in Manchester supports Manchester City. That's nonsense of the highest order. I guess it stems from the success that Manchester United have enjoyed over the last decade or so. Now, people tend to assume that anybody who supports United must obviously be a glory hunter.

But it's always been the way. How many kids started supporting Leeds when they were successful at the end of the 60s and early 70s? How many people started following Liverpool in the 80s when they were winning everything in sight?

Personally, I don't see the problem. If you live in Surrey and you want to support Manchester United then good for you. If you want to travel up from London to Old Trafford every Saturday then it's entirely your choice. I couldn't give a monkey's where you live or what you do with your time or your money. It doesn't happen with any other fans. If you're a Rochdale fan, say, and you live in Hampshire, no one cares in the slightest. They only hate you when your team's successful. I always say to people worry about who you support and let others do what they want to do.

When Chelsea won the league it was horrendous, suddenly everyone was interrogating you, it was like being confronted by the SS, 'How long have you been going?', 'When was your first match?', 'Did you go to Boro away?' It was madness. I felt like I was in a Mel Brooks movie. I even had a Chelsea fan the other day telling me that it's not the same at Stamford Bridge. 'I used to always be able to get a ticket but now it's always sold out.' No s***, Einstein. Two championships and several cups and more people want to come to the matches? Who'd have thought that? Listen, if Brentford started winning the Premiership every season, you try getting a ticket for Griffin Park. Important lesson: Just enjoy your success, because it won't last forever. Ask Liverpool fans!

EMBRACE
NEW TECHNOLOGY (AND USE IT TO ANNOY YOUR MATES)

One of the strangest things to happen to the life of the football fan in recent years is the advent of the text message. Before they came along, you could avoid your so-called mates when your team were losing but now as soon as Chelsea go one-nil down I get a barrage of texts from friends saying 'Get in!' or 'The Bubble's Burst'. More recently, a couple of my Gooner friends have been sending text messages which, when opened, burst into Kool & The Gang's 'Celebration' every time Chelsea lose.

The thing about this is that if your mates want to have a pop they can do it almost instantly now. They don't have to wait till you see them next or for you to finally pick up the phone. It's also put an end to the suspense you used to feel on those big match occasions like the last day of the season. Once upon a time, it would be the job of one man and a transistor radio on the terraces to relay the scores from all the other matches, now everybody knows immediately what is going on around the country.

But I like new technology, even though I spend a fortune texting my mates about football. Now, if I'm at a game and there's a contentious moment, I'll know whether the referee has made the right decision right away, not through any big screen video replay, but because my mates will text me and say 'That was a definite penalty' or 'That was never offside'. Before, you had to wait for the television highlights when you got home later that night to see if your suspicions were confirmed. Now, your mates will let you know there and then.

ENJOY **EVERY** MOMENT

I think some of the fondest memories I have in life are from the away day adventures I've had as a football fan. Those are the precious times when friendships are made and cemented, and when you begin to realise the true value of camaraderie. There's something special about getting up with a hangover at the crack of dawn on a Saturday and then driving to the other end of the country just to watch your team play. Mind you, there's also something just a little bit daft about it all too.

Trains, planes, automobiles – I've done them all. I've been on coach trips organised by pubs where you end up drunk within half an hour of setting off and find yourself desperate for the loo for the rest of the journey. Usually, these would also be coaches without toilets which, much to the driver's annoyance, meant several unscheduled stops on grass verges on the side of the M1 or wherever, when everybody would then pile off the coach and relieve themselves at the side of the motorway. Somebody once told me that their solution to the problem was to wee in a carrier bag, tie a knot in the top and then shove it through the skylight in the coach roof as you're speeding down the road. Invariably, though, the bag would burst and then all you would see is urine all running down the windows.

Going to away games on trains always seemed to be a bit scary. You were herded onto a train where half the seats were already missing and everybody was crowded into the other end. These were called 'Football Specials'. But there was nothing special about them. People would get more and more drunk as the journey went on, with all sorts of shenanigans going on. Every now and then you would get some mentalist saying 'Let's smash up the train!' while I would be staring down at my Diadora's questioning the logic of that statement, especially as we had to get home on the same train.

The only consolation was that you were with your own fans and in a way that what's made it so exciting. Getting off the train at Leeds or Manchester with thousands of other Chelsea fans gave you this real sense of community, of union. It's the most amazing feeling when you are travelling in those sorts of numbers. After all, you are all there for the same, single reason – to watch your team play.

Travelling by car was always the best though. I used to go with a bunch of mates who changed week by week, depending on who had enough cash to go. There was Chelly, Fat Phil (so-called because his name was Phil and he was fat), Mark and Pete. The only constant was Ginger and that was because he had a car.

Whenever we went away we would always bring some tunes with us for the journey because you could never rely on local radio stations playing anything decent. Trouble was, the stereo in Ginger's car – a battered red Sunbeam Alpine he called Boris with no indicators and no reverse gear – packed in one season, leaving the tape that was still jammed in it as the only thing we could play on our trips away. Had it have been one of our compilation tapes that wouldn't have been so bad but it wasn't. It was a tape with just two songs on; Madonna's 'Holiday' on one side and New Order's 'Blue Monday' on the other. So that's all we ever listened to as we made our way up and down the country, Madonna and New Order, endlessly on a loop, until the tape finally gave in.

Back in the day, Ginger (his real name is Stuart Clarke) was my best football mate. We went everywhere together to see Chelsea play, sharing the good times and the bad times. He was and still is one of the most passionate Chelsea fans I know. One time, Ginger turned up at my house and pleaded with me to go to Southampton with him to see Chelsea. I was still recovering from snapping a tendon in my finger and, to be honest, I didn't feel like going. But Ginger wouldn't let it lie. 'Don't let me down Tim,' he said. 'I've got you a ticket.' Reluctantly, I agreed and we set off for The Dell.

Eventually, we arrived at the ground and as we got out of his rust bucket I asked Ginger where my ticket was. 'Er, well,' he stammered, 'I haven't actually got any tickets.' What's more, we went to the ground and it was sold out. At that time there was a lot of trouble associated with Chelsea fans and the police formed a ring round us and refused to let us go just in case we turned into Charles Manson in Southampton town centre. My hand was all bandaged up so I pleaded with the police to let us go. But they wouldn't have it. So we spent ninety minutes sitting on a pavement outside The Dell listening to the crowd over the wall. Bloody Ginger. I could've killed him.

There was also a trip to Cardiff that could so easily have gone horribly wrong. Ginger and I arrived early and parked the car up.

We thought we were at the Chelsea end so paid at the nearest turnstile, went into the stand and soon realised we were in the wrong end. What made things worse was that I was wearing a brand new, hot off the press Sergio Tacchini ski jacket and jeans bleached from the knee down, which short of wearing a replica Chelsea kit was a clear sign that I wasn't a local.

A few comments here and a couple of nasty glances there and we decided that it was best to try and get moved. So I explained our predicament to a policeman and asked if he could move us into the Chelsea end at which point all the Cardiff fans started to smell a rat. But the policeman said no. I could here people asking 'Who the f*** are they?' and we were getting increasingly nervous, more and more worried. Meanwhile, a little group of angry men had formed behind us.

So I went back to the policeman and pleaded with him one more time. I think he could see the terror on my face and realised that things could well turn nasty and I was going to end up in A&E. So he went to check with his superior and eventually he came back and took us out the front of the home end, walked us round the pitch perimeter and back in front of the Chelsea fans who promptly burst into a chorus of 'Loyal Supporters'. For some reason, they assumed that me and Ginger were some hardcore fans who had tried to take the Cardiff end on our own when the truth was that we were cacking ourselves and had begged to be moved like big girls.

IF ALL ELSE FAILS, GIVE UP

I've had some brilliant times at football matches, and I recommend it to everyone, but not everyone is like me and I've often sat or stood in a football ground watching people go through pure pain and agony and I think to myself, Is it all worth it? Imagine these people who become frustrated football fans start hating their football clubs and bombard radio phone-in shows and chat rooms with their misery.

I once heard some great advice and it's very simple: If you're not enjoying yourself, don't go.

7

WOMEN
IN
FOOTBALL.

DISCUSS.

Let me start with a confession. I have always thought that women and football was, inherently, a bad combination. Now I'll hold my hands up and admit that's completely and utterly sexist but I have my reasons, some of which I'll go into later.

But it's not like I was brought up thinking that women and football were mutually exclusive. Far from it. When I was a kid my mum and dad used to watch football together. She even went with him to matches but my dad stopped taking her when she started getting a little too animated and began abusing the referees a bit too much for his liking. My nan was very much into football too. The trouble with her though was that she supported Leeds but then she decided to switch to supporting Liverpool instead. And then she denied point blank that she had ever followed Leeds. You can't do that.

Maybe it was the experience of witnessing my mum and my nan watch football that made me realise that women, for the most part, have a different emotional response to watching the game than we men.

Well, that and they don't *really* understand it…

THE TROUBLE WITH WOMEN'S FOOTBALL

I have noticed that over the last ten years or so that there are significantly more women involved in all aspects of football: in the media, at board level, in the players' canteen, etc. That, undeniably, is a good thing. But I must admit that in the early days of *Soccer AM* we all used to watch women's football and just absolutely wet ourselves. It was hysterical. Pure belly-laugh comedy.

In the last ten years, though, the standard of the women's game has improved dramatically. Today, you see some of the kids at the academies and their skills are phenomenal, they really are. But while the sport is growing, it is still a completely different game to the men's game. And that, I'm afraid, is down to the goalkeepers.

If you've ever watched a women's game you'll know that women goalies simply cannot jump. I have no idea why that may be the case, but they are absolutely hopeless. I said this once to one of the goalies at Charlton's ladies side and I thought she was going to punch my lights out. But it's true, if you aim for the top right hand corner or top left hand corner in a women's game, you will always score. They can't take goal kicks either. You watch. They'll always get the centre-half to trot back and take it for them, just so the ball will actually leave the penalty area.

I've always said that there are 20 footballers on the pitch and the two people who can't play football, the goalies, so imagine what women's goalies must be like. Sadly I think women's football in this country has taken a backwards step recently. I'm not talking about the skill levels, which is vastly improving as the years go on, but I'm talking about the set-up. The women's teams align themselves to the men's professional outfits. When the clubs decided to make cutbacks the first thing they did was take the money out of the women's teams and re-direct to men's reserve and youth teams. I believe there is only one professional women's team left, which is connected to Arsenal. Not that they probably want my advice, but if they want the sport to be taken seriously, they need to set up their own football clubs and grow the sport organically. Either that, or take up netball.

NEVER LET CHILDREN NEAR YOUR TREASURED POSSESSIONS

If you need more proof about the perils of women in football, let me tell you a little story. OK, so one of the *Soccer AM* boys had been out to interview the great Brazilian striker Rivaldo and had got him to sign a silver mini Nike football for me. It had taken pride of place at my house and whenever people came to visit, I just happened to mention it. 'Oh that, it's just a ball signed by Rivlado . . .'

My twin daughters wanted to give me a birthday present and kept asking me what I wanted so I told them that I really wanted a silver football, knowing full well that their mum would help them wrap up the one I had knocking around. Months later, I was sitting on the sofa watching a match on TV when my daughter Gracie came in. 'Daddy, I've found your ball,' she said, 'it was really dirty, Daddy, and had writing all over it, but I've managed to scrub it all off.' I was so horrified I actually started laughing in sheer disbelief.

'Why are you laughing Daddy?' she asked me.

'Because that was Rivaldo's autograph and you've wiped it off the football!' I replied. She started crying because she thought she'd done me a favour by washing off all the writing. Now, I ask you, would a son have done that? I know he would have had no respect for the autograph, but at least he would have been out in the garden kicking it about. Not cleaning it.

TREAT THE MISSUS WELL

Never let it be said that I am not romantic. There were many times when I suggested to my ex-wife that we take an impromptu weekend break to a luxurious destination on the Continent. One year we went to Rome, for example. Another time we went to Milan. The fact that both trips happened to coincide with the Rome and Milan derbies was entirely coincidental.

Later, when we were getting divorced, those trips tended to get brought up quite a bit. 'The only time you took me abroad,' she said, 'was when you took me to a bloody football match.' This was true, but as I always used to point out, football pays our bills. The same went for the TV: football was work, and took priority over soaps. And then there were the friends' weddings for which I wasn't able to go because I was too busy working, watching football on Sky. I do remember explaining once how important Bolton-Middlesbrough was to my career.

Strangely we're divorced now. It was funny, though, because she did admit, months later, that she enjoyed the football trips. Now, when she's out and about and blokes start talking to her about football, she slips it into the conversation that she's been to the Rome and Milan derbies and they're all dead impressed.

As a postscript to this, I always say to my daughters, 'Why do we have to watch football?' and they reply, 'Because it buys us clothes and food, Daddy.' They're going to make good wives!

NOT **ALL** WOMEN ARE THE SAME

Soccer AM had been running for a year or so when I got involved with the show. Back then it was an entirely different programme, much more serious, less knockabout. It was hosted by the DJ Russ Williams and the ex-footballer Gary Stevens, who were joined by a woman called Helen Chamberlain. I had been sent some tapes of her before I joined and decided that if I was going to make this the coolest show on the television then I was going to have to get rid of her. What, I asked myself, could she possibly know about football?

Then I met her and straight away I knew she had to stay. She was warm, funny and amazingly enthusiastic. She was also incredibly knowledgeable about the game and I knew we could do some great stuff together. Thankfully, it turned out to be one of my better decisions.

What's great about Helen is that she understands what her role in football is and the fans and the players love her for that. She is, for example, a champion of lower division football. She loves balls being pumped up into the box, with loads of people getting stuck in and the players getting their knees muddy and she's not afraid to admit it. I love the way she can take or leave European football and the way she still thinks football is a 'man's game'. Often, Adidas or Nike would ring Helen and ask her if she wanted their latest pair of boots and she just wouldn't get it. 'I'm a woman,' she would say. 'What on earth would I be doing playing football?'

But the truth is she can actually play a bit too. I remember she once got talked into playing at a Soccer Sixes tournament and it turned out she was the best player there. It didn't surprise me because she's good at everything; darts, pool, horse riding, she can do it all. She even won half a million dollars playing poker a couple of years back. Let's face it, as women go she's pretty cool.

TOOT CAMP

While we are talking about women on football pitches, there is an unwritten law that states that any woman under 40 that walks around the pitch must be subjected to a chorus of wolf whistles and then a 'Get your t**s out' chant. The thing is I believe that the women that do go on the pitch know full well this is going to happen – that's why they always wear high heels and full make-up.

WOMEN + T-SHIRT × FOOTBALL = SOCCERETTE

It was one of those ideas that I never thought I'd get away with but somehow I did. We needed to give away a t-shirt in a competition on *Soccer AM* and had to find someone to model it. So I started wondering whether we could actually get girls to parade up and down the studio wearing the shirts but somehow do it in a way that wouldn't leave me open to being labelled a sexist, a chauvinist or a pornographer. So we put it out there, even though it was a bit Readers' Wives, and let the people decide and it transpired that women loved it every bit as much as the men.

If you ever watch the show with a wife or girlfriend, though, you can bet that the item they were most interested in was the Soccerette section. Whereas men would wake up with a hangover from the night before and find some crumbs of comfort in a sexy girl in a tight t-shirt on their TV, the women would be far, far more critical, saying things like 'Doesn't she have fat ankles?' or 'Look at her split ends!' In short, the kind of things only women would ever notice.

Initially, it was hard to get girls to come on the show. But then why would they when all they'd be modelling was a big, baggy, black t-shirt? So we made the decision to change the shirt to a trendy, tight-fitting white t-shirt and soon the applications came pouring in. So we pushed it a bit further by making them wear short skirts as well and the floodgates just opened. In fact, the less politically correct the item was, the more popular it became among the ladies. It was absolutely astonishing.

As the years passed, we began to notice that some of the women who wanted to be a Soccerette were getting increasingly desperate to come on and they would send in photos of themselves in very little clothes in the kind of poses you usually see on the top shelf. Generally speaking, we didn't choose these girls not because of the nature of the photos but because when they did make it on the programme they invariably said the same thing. You could read them like a book. They liked clothes and shopping and going out and getting into nightclubs and they wanted to be a model and their hero was Jordan and they liked going on holiday and they did self-tanning and so on and so on. It was absolute nonsense and I was just horrified that all these women were like that.

What is funny about the Soccerette is when you get the photos sent in and you invite them in to the show. Then you see them in

You can see the delight on Robbie Fowler's face from meeting one of his idols.

My first-ever appearance at Wembley. Robbie Williams asked to sit next to me to get his profile up.

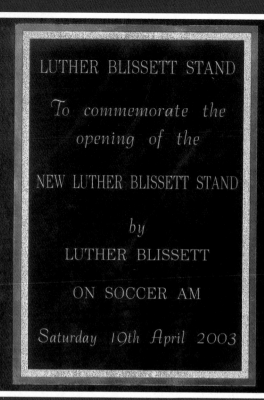

LUTHER BLISSETT STAND

To commemorate the
opening of the

NEW LUTHER BLISSETT STAND

by

LUTHER BLISSETT

ON SOCCER AM

Saturday 19th April 2003

I thought I'd better steal some mementos from *Soccer AM* when I left and this is one of them... I'm not sure whether they've noticed yet.

The fake Mickey Thomas £50 notes that we made up. My favourite bit of this is we have him pictured in a Chelsea kit.

Charity match at Rhyll, where I got to play with another one of my heroes, Joey Jones.

Gazza gave me this picture when he came on the show once. Reminds me of how brilliant he was for England.

An arty photo from the first-ever Badgers match.

The moment after Razor Ruddock nearly killed me on a football pitch.

Noel Gallagher entertaining us as he always did. Here he is playing the Wheel of Football.

All smiles in the tsunami charity line-up. Little did I know, not long after, Razor Ruddock was going to commit GBH on me.

Me laughing at Ray Winstone, as shy and retiring as always, coming out to play at Wembley.

Look at my disdain and Bradley's obvious delight at me having my picture taken in an Arsenal kit.

What can I say... 'Don't worry, it's only Ray Parlour.'

Ray Parlour

Ar
Millenniu

Having just secured the Premiership title at Old Trafford, the newly crowned champions had to rel
hosted the Cup Final against Chelsea who's team of overseas stars were capable of an upset. The (
needed. It was supplied by Ray Parlour whose magnificent long-range strike gave Cudicini no cha
enigmatic Freddie Ljungberg. Arsene Wenger's team had cor

- THE F.A. CUP

0
May 2002

Gary Brandham

...try and complete their historic third double in the F.A. Cup Final. Cardiff's Millennium Stadium ...t their best with the game evenly poised with chances at both ends. A moment of inspiration was ...this, Arsenal went on to win in style with a magnificent curling shot into the top corner from the ...put themselves firmly at the pinnacle of the English game.

The first match at the new Wembley and I was the first captain to lift a trophy there. Did I mention I scored?

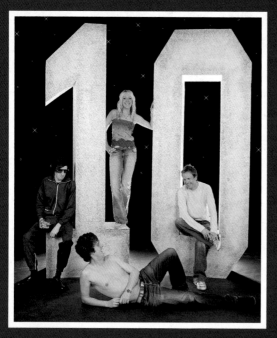

This was the actual match ball going to Wembley, with Jason McAteer and Bradley Walsh's initials on it.

To celebrate ten years of *Soccer AM* we all posed round a big number ten. Those marketing guys are geniuses, aren't they?

real life and the picture bears no relation to what they actually look like in person. It was like 'That is not you. That is nothing like you. It bears no resemblance to you. And how many years ago was this picture taken? You must have put on two stone.'

Unfortunately, we never had the budget to properly vet all the Soccerette applications so all we had to rely on was their photograph. By the time they came in for the show it was too late. They had to go on air. But you know what? They were often the funniest ones we had, even if it wasn't intentional.

Finally, while we're on the subject of Soccerettes I want to clear up a common misconception. There's a clip on the You Tube website that purports to be a Soccerette flashing her nether regions when she was on the show. While I agree that it looks fairly incriminating I feel duty bound to save the girl's blushes. What you can see when her skirt rides up is not her you know what but her knickers underneath her tights. She contacted us soon after it took off on the internet, pleading with us to take it off but it wasn't us that put it on there. Honest.

WHY THERE WILL **NEVER BE** A FEMALE REFEREE

You may recall that last season the Luton Town manager Mike Newell criticised the use of a lineswoman, Amy Rayner, in one of his team's matches. 'We have a problem in this country with political correctness and bringing women into the game is not the way to improve refereeing and officialdom,' he said. 'It's absolutely beyond belief. If you start bringing in women, you have big problems.'

Now I'm not one to criticise women. After all, some of the

best times I have ever had have been with women. But Newell's comment got me thinking about whether the gender of a match official is of any relevance whatsoever. It also led me to ask some pretty hard-hitting questions. Would a female official be more lenient if she fancied the player that had transgressed? Would she be less tolerant of bad language? Would she favour the team with the nicest kit? And would she be too preoccupied with what conditioner Robbie Savage is using these days?

Joking aside, there seems to be a bit of a contradiction in the attitude of the authorities on female match officials. On one hand it is OK to use them as linesmen (or rather lineswomen) but have the FA, the Premiership, UEFA or FIFA ever appointed a woman as a referee? No they haven't. Which, in my book, means they all trust women to officiate at games about as much Mike Newell does.

SHE'S THE BOSS

When I was growing up, there were no women involved in football at all. Women used to watch it, but their only involvement at club level would be to make the tea and the sandwiches. Things have moved on dramatically in the last ten years, and only the other day I was discussing the unthinkable with my friends. Could there ever be a female manager in the Premier League? Initially I thought, of course not, but then as one of my friends pointed out, at the turn of the century, could any man have envisaged a woman, Margaret Thatcher, becoming Prime Minister? And also, could we have ever envisaged a female commentator? Well, last year, that dream/nightmare became a reality for one week. Now I'm not anti-change and I'm not anti-women, but I found it really hard to listen to. I think it's going to take a good few years yet before we all feel comfortable with this.

8

THE POWER OF TELEVISION

occer AM was never a negative show. As far as I'm concerned, it's too easy to simply hammer everything. I remember during the first series of the show I'd told a cheap, lazy gag at the expense of Spurs striker Jason Dozzell. That night, I went out to a club and Jason was in there too. He came over to me and said: 'Do you want to have a pop at me on TV do you?' I thought he was going to punch my lights out. So I sort of laughed sheepishly and walked away.

But then it really hit me that I may have actually offended this bloke and I didn't even know him. So I went over to him and apologised and he said: 'No, I'm sorry, it's your job. But when you say things like that my kids hear, my wife hears, my friends see it, all the fans see it and then you get jeered by the fans. It doesn't help.' I suddenly realised the sort of power you possess on TV and radio to mercilessly slaughter footballers, who are just trying to do their job, sometimes in very difficult circumstances, and all they get is the usual negative spin from the media. I started analysing this a lot more and I began to see the hypocrisy of some fat journalist saying Beckham had lost it, or some moderately-talented ex-pro criticising a player in his newspaper column. I decided I was not going to be part of the whole circus and was determined to rise above it all and get people enjoying their football again.

So from that day on, I went on *Soccer AM* every week and was positive about everything, I wanted players to feel that they didn't have to watch the show from behind a pillow or through their fingers. I wanted the players to enjoy it as much as the fans. I now count many footballers as my friends and I've had some great times with them.

BLOODY RAY PARLOUR...

It was the 2002 FA Cup Final at the Millennium Stadium. Chelsea v Arsenal. Me and Arsenal fan Bradley Walsh had been asked to do the Fanzone Commentary of the game by Sky and were only too happy to oblige. Can you believe it? I was a Chelsea fan, and here I was, commentating on the biggest domestic cup final in the world, with my team playing. I was made up. When the game got underway, Bradley started taking it quite seriously. Deep down, I suspect he fancied doing it for a full-time career and maybe he thought it was some kind of audition. But to give him his credit he was pretty good at it. Anyway, the game was still goalless after 70 or so minutes when Ray Parlour picked the ball up in the Chelsea half. As he moved forwards, Bradley started getting excited so I said 'Don't worry, it's only Ray Parlour' at which point Parlour spanks the ball from twenty-five yards and it flies into the back of the net. One nil to the Arsenal. As Bradley went mental, though, I just held my head in my hands. At the time I didn't think too much about it and it was only after the game when Chelsea had lost that I began to realise what I'd said. Unbeknown to me they had already shown the Fanzone highlights on Sky and as I walked into the players' lounge, the Sky presenter Richard Keys came up to me and said: 'It's only Ray

Parlour, Tim!' Then Alan Shearer comes over. 'Don't worry Tim,' he says, 'It's only Ray Parlour!' Then it's George Graham's turn. 'It's only Ray Parlour Tim!'

Suddenly this one throwaway comment got out of control. Everywhere I went complete strangers were just coming up to me saying 'Hey Tim, it's only Ray Parlour, it's only Ray Parlour.' Even the Arsenal club shop had a sign up in the window. The next time Chelsea and Arsenal played at Stamford Bridge, all the Arsenal fans had even made up a song about me and what I'd said about Ray Parlour and I was just like 'Oh my God, they've actually sung a song about it!' OK, it wasn't the kind of song you'd want your mother to hear, in fact it was incredibly insulting, but they had gone out of their way to take the p*** out of me and I had made it into a football chant. The impact of my gaffe, live on TV, astonished me. Arsenal fans still, to this day, haunt me with the words, 'It's only Ray Parlour.'

Some time after it happened, I finally got to speak to Ray Parlour about the whole incident and he was really good about it. In fact, he thought it was hilarious. He even sent me a big picture of him scoring his FA Cup Final goal with the words 'It's only Ray Parlour' written on it.

STAR QUALITY

Serge Pizzorno from Kasabian must be one of the coolest people on the planet. Not only is he in one of the best bands that Britain has got but he also has a permanent place in the annals of *Soccer AM* as the man who scored the most audacious goal in the rich and varied history of our car park game at the end of the show.

Often, when we had celebrities take part, they would take it really easy so as not to embarrass themselves. Not Serge. When it was his turn to try, he trotted up in his leather jacket and his winkle pickers, chipped the ball up into the air and then spanked a volley straight through the hole. Confident isn't the word. Now whenever the band are on tour he finds himself being stopped in the strangest places by people who just want to talk about the moment he hit that volley on *Soccer AM*.

I often wondered whether he got lucky that day but when I ended up playing with him at Wembley I realised it wasn't, because he showed that day that he's got a lot of other tricks in his locker and scored yet another cracker. He picked up the ball on the left hand side of the box, flicked the ball onto his right foot and then curled a beauty right into the corner. There's no denying it, Serge has definitely got something and I have nothing but respect for the bloke, even if Noel Gallagher reckons that he is now more famous for that moment than he is for his music. This is probably true. Again, the power of telly.

Now I've mentioned Noel, he loves his footy, and has come on *Soccer AM* many a time, but was always unlucky at the end and never got the ball through the hole. It seemed he was always destined for failure. Then, two years ago, on Cup final day, Noel finally slotted the ball through the hole in Wembley, and fell to his knees in jubilation. Yes, Serge's goal was the greatest, but I think Noel's celebration spoke volumes. I also want to go on record to say that he is, quite simply, the ultimate entertainer. With the rest of the rock and roll industry, all you ever seem to get are ridiculous demands and unfounded attitude; bands and artists will only come on if they get to plug their single, album or tour. Not Noel. He just chips up because he fancies it.

It's the same with Ray Winstone. He would come on the programme when he wanted just to have a chat about West Ham, not because he's got a new film coming out. That, in my opinion, is the hallmark of a real celebrity and any wannabes should really take a leaf out of their books. I've also had the pleasure of playing with Ray a couple of times at Wembley, and even though he's getting on a bit now to be playing football, he's not bad, and even if he wasn't I wouldn't tell him to his face, because I think I'd end up in the bottom of the Thames.

TABLE FOR TWO

I've had the pleasure of playing Gazza on a few occasions at table tennis. We had first played at Chris Evans's house once and, I admit it, he had absolutely trounced me. In fact, it was the biggest thumping I'd ever suffered. He was very, very good and when you couple that with his in-built desire to win at everything he ever does, it proved to be too much for me. He's just one of those natural sportsmen, brilliant at everything. It was only after he'd beaten me that I was told that he'd won several table tennis competitions back in Newcastle.

So the next time he came on *Soccer AM*, I challenged him to a return match only this time I would be playing as 'The Ping Pong Prince'. And, what's more, it would be live on the show. Now, for whatever reason, Gazza went to pieces. He suddenly became really nervous and whenever the ball dropped to the floor he would chase around the studio desperately trying to pick it up. You could just tell that he was flustered.

Anyway, I ended up getting my revenge and beating him. To be honest, I was little embarrassed because he is a much, much better player than me. After the show I asked him whether he was as nervous as he looked. 'I was really nervous,' he confessed. 'I could play football in front of a hundred thousand people and I would be completely at home, but doing that was impossible.'

To this day he still can't believe that he lost to the Ping Pong Prince. Personally I think it was less to do with my ability and more the result of the way TV can make people, even world famous footballers, freeze.

EARLY DOORS

Before I became the international television personality you know and love today, I used to work as an outside broadcast (OB) producer for The Big Breakfast, Channel 4's early morning magazine show. This was at a time when football didn't really have the glamour and mass appeal that it does today and, try as I might, it was almost impossible to shoehorn any football in the programme. So me and a colleague, Simon Howley, decided to make a concerted effort to get more football into the OBs.

I finally made a breakthrough when I arranged for the show's presenter, Richard Awford, to take penalties against Liverpool's central defender John Scales. It was the first time I had met John Scales and what a brilliant man he was. More importantly, it was the first time I had been on the pitch at Anfield and it was the best thing ever.

Soon after, I did a deal with Manchester United wherein I would agree to promote their newly opened club museum in return for me doing some filming with the players. Now we were getting somewhere. So there I was hoping for Roy Keane, or maybe Mark Hughes to come and help us out on the Old Trafford pitch and instead they brought out these two kids who I'd never seen before. But as time was against us and this was live TV we had no option but to go with them. So we cut to Richard and he asked one of the lads his name. 'Gary Neville' came the reply. Then he asked the next boy. 'David Beckham,' he said. 'So what sort of things do you do in training,' continued Richard.

The boys shrugged. 'Just kick the ball around and stuff,' said Gary. I really felt for the lads. They were both shy young men who had just broken through and you could tell that though they were both excited they were also really nervous. Little did we know that they would both end up captaining club and country. Somewhere that footage must exist. This is David Beckham's first-ever TV appearance and I've always been surprised that no one has ever dug it out.

Still nobody really cared about football at The Big Breakfast. Even a mass turnout at the Riverside Stadium failed to convince them that we should do more football. When we heard that Juninho was about to sign for Boro we decided to turn a Middlesbrough estate into Brazil, not just to make Juninho feel at home but to give the fans a little taste of the samba lifestyle too. So we took the OB truck up to Middlesbrough and began setting up. We got some samba music on the stereo, we had typical Brazilian food and a bunch of samba girls in bikinis from a local modelling agency. How some of them were on a modelling agency's books I'll never know, but they were keen and that's what mattered. We even handed out sombreros, even though they're technically Mexican, and not really Brazilian at all. Usually, we only had a maximum of about 30 people who turned up at our OBs. By the time we went on air, there must have been a thousand people crowded around us, enjoying the festivities at the Riverside.

That day made me realise just how special the North East of England is. They weren't so enthusiastic at The Big Breakfast, though. Despite my repeated calls for more football items on the show, they just didn't seem interested. Not even a thousand Boro fans and a troupe of samba girls in bikinis could convince them there was a future in football. It was time to move on, so I wrote a letter to Sky Sports and the rest is history.

RAZOR'S REVENGE

The power of TV can spectacularly backfire on you though, as I experienced first-hand. It was during a live televised charity game at Anfield that I finally got my comeuppance from Neil 'Razor' Ruddock. It was a celebrity team versus Liverpool legends. Leading up to the match I had been winding him up constantly on *Soccer AM*. I said, 'We're playing against a team of Liverpool legends… and Razor Ruddock's playing as well.' Just to put the boot in, I added, 'I'm going to run rings around Razor Ruddock… but it'll take me half an hour to get round him because he's so big.' Anyway, before the game I met up with him and as we shook hands he just looked at me and smiled. That's all. When I got to our dressing room I realised why. There on a piece of paper on top of my shirt were the words:

'LOVEJOY YOU'RE A **** – YOU ARE GOING TO DIE, RAZOR'.

When the game got underway, it wasn't long before Razor got his revenge. I picked up the ball in the opposition half and the next thing I know I was in a crumpled heap on the floor in absolute agony. As I lay on the turf, I looked up and all I saw was

Razor running off with his hands in the air milking the crowd for all his worth.

I have to tell you, it genuinely did hurt, and at the moment of impact I honestly thought I was going to have to go to hospital. I think I realised after the match that all ex-pros have got that competitive mentality and have no choice but to hammer me for being cocky. Whenever I watch celebrity vs professionals football matches, when the celebrities are giving it large before the match, I always think, 'That's a bad move. You're going to get done.' And invariably, they do.

ANTHONY HUTTON KILLED CELEBRITY FOOTBALL

I've always thought that you can only tell what a person is really like in real life when you've seen them play football. There is something strange about being on a football pitch that makes it impossible for anyone to pretend to be someone or something else. If you're a hard man you're not going to turn into Glenn Hoddle. Likewise, if you're absurdly talented and creative, you won't be able to turn yourself into David Batty. It can't be done.

It's no different in the world of celebrity football. There are great players, half-decent players and players that really shouldn't bother. Some of the best ones I've shared a pitch with are Phil Daniels, Bradley Walsh, Ralf Little, MC Harvey, Jonathan Wilkes, Nicky and Brian from Westlife, Philip 'Tinhead' Olivier. I apologise to any of my celebrity friends I have left off this list but that's the problem. There's too many 'celebrity' football matches now and too many so-called 'celebrity' players.

Back when I started playing there was a man called Steve Sutherland who worked at Charlton and he used to organise the celebrity games before the Charity Shield and the Carling Cup and when he called you felt privileged to have been asked. People were chosen on their celebrity status. You had big rock Gods like Rod Stewart, pop stars like Robbie Williams, soap stars who had tens of millions watching them every week and household names like Chris Evans. I was lucky enough to sneak in because I did a football show. These were always good fun and you felt special to be involved. But then when the Sky programme 'The Match' (a team of ex-professionals playing a team of celebrities) came along it was no longer OK to be famous, you also had to be good at football. Even though the first one was great, it signalled the death of celebrity football. Suddenly instead of high-profile stars, they were fielding reality TV stars like Anthony Hutton in a vain attempt to even up the teams. Now, every other week you turn on the TV and there's another pro-celebrity game on in aid of charity, not to mention ratings and saving people's careers. I now get asked to play in games like this at least once a month and I'm very sceptical about any of these pro-celebrity style programmes.

I hereby officially declare 'celebrity football' is dead. Unless I get asked to play at Wembley, Stamford Bridge, Anfield, Old Trafford, Emirates, the Nou Camp, the San Siro, the Maracana . . . basically I'll play anywhere.

THERE'S **NO** BUSINESS LIKE **SHOW** BUSINESS . . .

Whilst we're talking about celebrity football, when you are first offered the opportunity to play in so-called 'celebrity' charity games you can't help but feel a little flattered. In the early days of *Soccer AM* when nobody really knew who I was I was approached by the entertainer Jess Conrad to play in his Showbiz XI team and I thought 'why not?', especially as it was for charity.

The all-star Showbiz XI dated back to the 1950s and in its heyday had featured the cream of British entertainment playing for the side. Things had changed by the time I arrived on the scene. God bless Jess and his team for going to the trouble and organising these games but the day I played was the most embarrassing day of my life.

I knew it was going to be bad when they got a John Major lookalike to kick the game off. As I looked across the team the only 'celebrities' I recognised was that ginger bloke who used to do some Saturday night television a few years ago (no, not Chris Evans) and someone who I think may have been in a Kentucky Fried Chicken advert. Mind you, I was hardly A-list either. At one stage I was near the touchline and one of the spectators started shouting to me. 'Mate! Mate! Mate! Who are you?' 'Tim Lovejoy,' I replied. He looked blank. 'And who is everyone else in the team? I've never seen any of you before in my life.' After that humiliation, I decided that it wasn't really fair to charge people to watch games that purported to be showbiz matches but clearly weren't. It was like going to a testimonial game when you've been told that Maradona or Cruyff are going to play and then you get there and, surprise, surprise, they've made their excuses. It wasn't really fair. That's why we decided never to charge people for coming to watch my team The Badgers. How could we? But you know what, it was a policy that worked. Sometimes we would have two or three thousand people turn up to see us play. That's more than League Two sides get and to me at least, those games felt like playing proper football matches. There would be people on the sidelines chanting horrible things at you. I'd get players purposefully kicking me or trying to nutmeg me. The buzz was amazing. I loved it.

9

REFEREES I LOVE

10

UNWRITTEN RULES OF FOOTBALL

Anyone can read the FIFA handbook and know that there are seventeen laws governing the game. However, there are laws that are not in the referee's bible, and the only way to obtain this knowledge is to watch copious amounts of football, either on the terraces or on the telly. Luckily for you, I'm going to impart my knowledge to you in true Obi-Wan Kenobi style. So, young Jedi Knight, these are the unwritten rules of football . . .

When a team is losing a game by two goals or more and they get a goal back, the goalscorer must grab the ball from the back of the opposition net, stick it under his arm, sprint directly back to the centre-spot without showing a flicker of emotion and place the ball on the centre-spot ready for the resumption of play. If the goalkeeper attempts to prevent the goalscorer from retrieving the ball then the dispute will be settled with a juvenile scuffle in the six-yard box. David Platt was the undisputed king of this. He once scored four goals for England in a game against San Marino at Wembley and even after his fourth he was still picking the ball out of the net and running back to the centre circle with his chest pushed out.

Now that's professionalism.

When a player unleashes a shot that streaks wide of the post or hits the woodwork they will always look up to the stadium's big video screen to see how close they were but will do so in a sly, sneaky way to make it look like they're not actually that bothered. Frank Lampard is a master at this.

Referees will never award a penalty against the champions at their home ground.

When a player is awarded a free-kick, they must throw the ball forward with back spin to grab themselves an extra few yards.

When a goalkeeper makes a spectacular save and is congratulated by his team-mates he must furiously usher them away, pretending that the save meant absolutely nothing to him.

If a player goes down injured and the team in possession stops play by kicking the ball out, the crowd MUST applaud when the other team gives the ball back from the restart, even though failure to do so would be nothing other than cheating of the worst kind.

When a manager is asked about a controversial refereeing decision in post-match conferences, they must always say 'I don't want to get myself into trouble . . .' before delivering a lengthy monologue about just how bad the official in question was and then receiving an FA charge/fine soon after.

If a player has spent any time playing in Italy, every decision that goes against him, he must put his hands together in a prayer position and beg the ref to change his mind like a six-year-old boy.

When your team gets drubbed 5–0, it also has to chuck it down so that you get soaked all the way home. No team ever loses 5–0 on a sunny day.

If you commit a foul you can hassle the referee without fear of caution as long as you place your hands behind your back.

In the fortnight before the new season, players of the deposed champions must say things like 'we want our title back – it hurts like hell' or 'it's only on loan' whenever they are interviewed by the media.

If your team is winning and you are in the dying moments of a game you are entitled to waste time by taking the ball over to the corner flag and sticking your backside out to shield the ball.

If you take the ball to the corner flag to waste time at the end of a match, the opposition players are allowed to kick seven shades of s*** out of you with the kind of challenge that would ordinarily result in a red card.

If a defender commits a two-footed foul on an opposition player, he can plead for leniency with the referee by making the shape of an imaginary ball with his hands.

If you are a footballer you must put the words 'to be fair' in every answer to journalists' question. That said, it is not going to make it fair by putting the word 'fair' in.

In post-match interviews, it is your duty as a player to use 'Erm . . .' at the beginning of every sentence.

If you're a footballer who has been invited on to Sky Sports as a guest pundit, you must wear the biggest tie you can lay your hands on, even if it hasn't been in fashion for years.

If you are a footballer and you have just scored one of the goals of the season you must not acknowledge this in post-match interviews. You must always say that it was the 'three points that were most important.' Even in a Cup match.

On World Cup duty, it is necessary for the England players to insert song lyrics into any interview they do.

The crowd must abuse anyone who walks on the pitch who isn't a player, unless they are a former player/legend in which case they must absolutely be applauded.

If you are an away fan at a big game, you must stand throughout the duration of the game even though you have a perfectly good seat. Furthermore, when the person on the public address system asks you to sit down, you are obliged to ignore them.

If you're the manager of a top Premiership team you must make three tactical substitutions during the match just to show what a tactical mastermind you are.

If you are standing behind the goal and the opposition are awarded a penalty at your end, you must wave your arms maniacally around as it's being taken. This doesn't actually work, but at least makes you feel like you're doing your bit.

If you are attending the first home game of the new season, you are obliged to mention how good the pitch looks to those around you.

The lower down the league structure you go, the longer the throw-ins must be. In the Premiership, for instance, throw-ins never tend to be any longer than two yards, three at most, and usually consist of one player throwing the ball to a team-mate who then cushions a volley back to the thrower. They start getting longer in the Championship, and by the time you reach League Two the throw-ins are just missiles launched from wherever into the opposition penalty area.

To be considered a good centre-half, you have to have played at least 45 minutes of a match with blood gushing from bandages wrapped around your head.

When an away team wins a corner, the home fans in that part of the stadium must make offensive and sexually-suggestive hand gestures behind the player's back as he prepares to take the kick.

Any players in the penalty area awaiting a corner kick must grapple with each other as if the corner is about to be taken that very second.

All British teams that have to pre-qualify for the Champions League must start their campaigns with an away match in a former Soviet bloc state, and journalists have to comment on the 1,000-mile round trip/artificial turf/subzero temperatures rather than the opposition team.

Any haircut seen in the Premier League will still be widely visible in League One two seasons later, when it's no longer fashionable.

If a team has a child prodigy, the manager must say that he is protecting him by not allowing him to talk to the media. This allows journalists to pursue him everywhere and pick apart every detail of his life.

When a player from the lower leagues is attracting interest from a Premier League club, he will always tell reporters, 'I'm very happy at Grimsby/Port Vale/Northampton Town.' At the end of the season, he will move.

Managers with a lengthening injury list will always start interviews with the words, 'I'm not going to discuss injuries,' and then proceed to talk in-depth about every single injured player in the squad.

When physios come on the pitch to treat a player, they must sprint as fast as their little legs can carry them.

When one of the big teams suffers a poor result, the manager is obliged to blame it on (a) international duty; (b) playing in Europe; or (c) fixture congestion.

When a player is sent off he has a ten-second window where he can shot, swear, push and generally berate anyone in the vicinity without fear of further punishment.

And finally, remember . . .

The referee is always, always biased against your team.

11

BRING ON THE BADGERS!

I t all began one day on London's Hampstead Heath. I was walking along with one of my ex-girlfriends. Something wasn't right. It wasn't her. It was me. I was restless, irritable and in a really foul mood. I felt like a dog that wasn't being exercised. I wanted to play football, but as a television presenter with his career on the up, I was just far too busy to play come the weekend. It was bugging me big time. When I had started doing *Soccer AM* I was playing at Sarrat FC but it was killing me. Trying to work all week, getting up early for the show and then playing football afterwards was just plain knackering. About half way through that first year at *Soccer AM* I realised that a) it was virtually impossible for me to carry on playing, and, b) it may be more advantageous for me and the show if I started going to Stamford Bridge to watch Chelsea again. Purely for professional reasons, of course. This was actually a hard decision, as I prefer playing to watching.

When I had started playing Saturday football, rather than Sunday League, I had done so for a number of reasons. Sunday, for one, was day off, my release. Sunday was the day when I recovered from the week (and from Saturday night). And, besides, from my experience the standard of Sunday League football was also inferior to that played on Saturday due largely to being bladdered the night before. All people ever wanted to do was kick lumps out of each other or start fights and that wasn't for me.

146

So faced with the prospect of not playing eleven-a-side football at all, I decided that the only way to satisfy my craving was by starting my own football team. It was a great idea. I would get some of my mates and some of the guys from the show and set up a side to play matches not in some weekend London league but around the country as and when challenged.

But first of all, we needed a name, something that filled the opposition with fear, something that reeked of history, tradition and quality. A burrowing mammal of the weasel family. Yes, the badger. Helen Chamberlain was from Torquay and we had always said on the show that all she ever drank was Badger Juice so we decided that in Helen's honour we would call our crack new football outfit 'The Mighty Badgers'.

Being 'The Badgers' we naturally played in black and white kit, black shorts and white socks, made by Bukta. Not the manufacturer of choice for Europe's elite but in fairness it was one of the best kits I've ever played in and the shorts were great. We had socks ties too like the ones Leeds made famous in the 1970s. How cool was that? And, in keeping with our flash new kit, we all pledged to play football that was attractive and free-flowing, skilful and honourable. Or at least, that was theory.

Our next challenge was finding opponents so I started appealing on *Soccer AM* for any team that fancied their chances. We didn't want a fee or any special treatment and we didn't want anyone to have to pay to come and see us (although they could take a bucket round for charity if they liked). All we asked of any of our potential opponents was that there was somewhere to go for a drink and a bite to eat afterwards. Suddenly the offers came flooding in from all over the country and the team we chose for our first opponents was a club in Leicestershire called Rutland

Rovers. It turned out to be a momentous day. While the game was good – we won 3–1 after trailing at half time (goals by Westy and a couple by Paul Harwood) – the drink up afterwards was better and the coach trip home topped the lot. There was drinking and singing, laughing and joking. It was a proper day out. There was no stopping the Mighty Badgers after that. We started travelling all over the country, like a football version of the Harlem Globetrotters. We even ended up playing against ex-pro teams, which in turn led to some ex-players turning out for the Badgers as well. Mickey Thomas soon became a firm favourite for the team as did the Liverpool defenders Alan Kennedy and Phil Neal. We had John Wark playing for us, John Beresford, Warren Barton and Keith O'Neill. We also had Paul Dalglish playing for us, even though he hadn't retired. Then we had Gaz Whelan, the drummer from the Happy Mondays, who would just hug the right touchline throughout the entire game.

We definitely never lacked for quality loan signings.

John Wark was something else. The first time he turned out for the Badgers I asked him if he wanted to play at the back, knowing full well that he had started his career upfront but moved back to defence as he got older. He just shrugged and said 'yeah' before adding, 'but if we're losing at half time I'll just go up and score a few goals.'

By the time the interval arrived we were 3–0 down so John came up to me and suggested he go back upfront and score some goals. And here's why John Wark is a giant of a man. Within three minutes of the restart, we were level and he had bagged the lot. On the outside, I was congratulating myself on such an inspired tactical change but on the inside I was beating myself up for sticking him at the back in the first place.

It was amazing to see someone like John Wark grabbing a game by the scruff of the neck and single-handedly changing it; it just shows that when you know what you are doing as a striker it can make a real difference. You stick me up front and I have no idea what I am doing but witnessing people like John Wark play you see that when they get half a yard the ball is in the back of the net.

The problem with playing with the pros was that there was always an awkward moment before each match which used to make me cringe. I was player-manager and captain, so it was up to me to pick the team and do the pre-match tactics and rousing speech. It was so embarrassing – I'd be standing there with all these pros who'd played for club and country and listened to the greats like Bob Paisley and now they were listening to me. I used to try and get out of it but pros being pros, they always said, 'It's your team, you're the gaffer, you do the talking.' I have to say they were all brilliant about it, always listened and gave me the occasional piece of advice as I was going along. If only the regular Badgers were as disciplined as them!

It was the regulars that made the Badgers the formidable outfit that they were. Apart from me, the main Badger and vice-captain was John Fendley, aka Fenners, who was also on free-kicks. We had Matty Coppock ('Copcat') with his sweet left foot; in the centre of defence we had Matt Milan (that's not his real name but he's a male model…) and we had Knoxy (as in Fort Knox, real name Dave Reynolds). We had Steve 'The Kid' Janson who was from Glasgow; we had Tony 'Turbo' Trafford, the little midfield maestro; we had Nick The Greek, so called because he was called Nick and he came from Greece, Mike 'Lloyd' Lloyd', Paul 'Leachy' Leach, Ben 'Westy' West, Neville 'Cotte' Cotte, Gary 'Kingy' King, and up front we had Dougie Bruce, another Scot, who is possibly one of the best payers I have ever played with. There was also Phil 'Nasher' Nash who only ever really helped to make the numbers up but got in because he is the funniest bloke anyone's ever met.

And then there is Fenners' mate from Scarborough and the Badger's goalkeeper, Sea Dog. His commitment to the cause was so deep, so massive that not only did he travel from Scarborough to all of our games but he even had a tattoo of the Badgers' club crest done on his arm. The bloke was just mad for that team.

These were the main Badgers' stalwarts but to be honest we operated a rotation system long before Rafa Benitez used one. The only difference was ours was based on who was hungover and who wasn't. That team travelled far and wide to meet their adoring public, and even their hate-filled, booing public. There was one game we played in Manchester near Cheadle Hulme where we had to run through this little housing estate to get to the pitch and it was so intimidating it made Galatasaray look like Brentford. Well, that's a slight exaggeration, but then again I am writing a book. As soon as we got on the pitch this chorus of boos rang out across the ground. It was a really uncomfortable atmosphere. We had always been used to ultra-friendly receptions where the home team went out of their way to make us feel welcome. Now we were genuinely scared.

For the most part, though, the Badgers away days were brilliant. It was genuinely like playing proper football matches. There would be people on the sidelines chanting horrible things at you. I'd get players purposefully kicking me or trying to nutmeg me. I loved it. One of the most memorable trips was up to the north-east to play at the home of the FA Cup giantkillers Blythe Spartans. That day 5,000 people turned up to watch us play, one of which happened to be the former England manager Bobby Robson. Yet again, I didn't get discovered but he did say that I wasn't 'a bad player' and I've never let anyone forget it. Sadly, that was based on my first-half performance. The second half wasn't as good and Bobby gave the man of the match award to Fenners. It was the same story when we played John Aldridge and the Tranmere Rovers coaching squad. We were goalless at half-time and I was furious. So I started my team talk and told everybody to stop thinking of them as professional footballers, stop paying them so much respect and to take the game to them. 'Look at Aldridge,' I raged. 'He's lost it. He's got nothing left to offer.'

Five minutes into the second half and the scoreline was Tranmere Rovers Coaches 3 Mighty Badgers 0. John Aldridge hat-trick. After having a stinker in the first half, Aldo had moved up several gears and everything he hit went in. His power and accuracy was phenomenal. That evening we went out in Liverpool and had a great time. We even bumped into Robbie Fowler. It was one of those nights when nobody wanted to go home. And, as it transpired, we didn't. All night, our coach driver kept telling us 'Ten minutes lads and we're going home,' and we were like 'whatever'. Eventually we got back to the car park and the coach had gone. Sick of waiting, the driver had cleared off back to London, taking all our stuff with him.

So our minds had been made up and that was it, we were out for the night. We ended up staying in the Adelphi Hotel but could only get two rooms, one of which had two people in it and the other which had fourteen in. Every single inch of that floor was covered with drunken, blabbering, stinking men. It was like a hospital field tent from 'Nam – casualties everywhere. And the biggest was me. That morning I woke up with a dreadful case of food poisoning. I was sitting on the toilet, whilst simultaneously puking in the basin, which was no mean feat. The problem with being one of the lads in the team, however, is that rather than leaving me to suffer in peace, one of our friends called Eggbot, decided to barge down the door and take pictures of me on his mobile phone.

MY PENALTY HELL

My penalty record with The Badgers is something that has brought a terrific amount of entertainment to many, many people over the years. But not for me, obviously.

And yet it had all started so well. I had scored with my first three spot kicks and began to feel really confident with taking them. Then I missed one, then another, then another. Before I knew it I'd missed five on the bounce. I was fast becoming a standing joke. What made it worse was that nobody ever took me to one side and suggested I should, you know, let someone else have a go. If anything, the more I missed the more everyone wanted me to take them just for the comedy value. It became such a hideous thing for me that I used to stand there in front of the goal and think for ages about what I was going to do. Suddenly, from being supremely confident, now the goalkeeper was looking enormous and the goal tiny. It actually gave me some idea of how every England player feels during shoot-outs at the World Cup or the European Championship, even though there were only two or three thousand people in the ground. In fact, I don't how anyone could ever take a penalty in a World Cup match. There must be so much pressure. No wonder Zidane was sick against us before taking his in Euro 2004.

THE BADGERS
– WHERE ARE THEY NOW?

A lot of people ask me whether the Mighty Badgers are still going, especially as I've now left *Soccer AM* and so many of that legendary side have now got married and had kids. The truth is, some of us went out the other night and like the Blues Brothers, we've seen the light. So talks are afoot and we're thinking about a world tour at a football ground near you soon.

MANA

12

GERS

In my 12 years of being involved with football, the job of football manager has gone from being one not unlike that of a used car salesman to the almost CEO level that is today. The other big change is, where once they were all British, like the playing staff, some of the best managers now are foreign. The stress managers are under defies belief. Take the cases of Arsene Wenger, Alex Ferguson and Rafa Benitez. These are three of the most successful managers in world football but they're now in the ridiculous position whereby if they don't win the League or a major trophy each and every season, their jobs are on the line. This is supposedly what happened to Mourinho when he only delivered two cups the season before (FA and Carling Cups). That is crazy. In fact, it occurred to me that the Premiership is actually now more about the managers than it is the teams these days. When Arsenal play Man Utd, it's Wenger v Fergie. These men are so important, so vital, that, if anything, they should be paid more than the players, not less. The manager's job has changed so dramatically because of the three subs' rule – in the past they picked eleven players and were pretty much stuck with them for ninety minutes. Now they can make three changes from a squad of five (or seven in Europe), meaning they have to be tactical geniuses, and the pressure has grown.

Make no mistake, being a manager is a tough job, although some clubs, like mine, are trying to free up their managers to do what they do best. Indeed, one of the reasons that Chelsea have prospered in recent years is not simply because of Roman Abramovich's billions but because the way he has used his money to restructure the club and employed the very best people he can in the key positions, thereby removing some of the day-to-day pressure on the coach.

You may think differently but Roman Abramovich does not want to run Chelsea FC. That's why he has got experts in to run each and every department. That means someone to take over the PR, someone to run the medical department and decide if a player is fit or not and someone to conduct transfer negotiations. After all, what does an ex-footballer know about the legal ramifications of a multi-million pound contract?

The way I see it, managers should be responsible for running team affairs and nothing else while the overall management of the football club should be down to a Chief Executive. These are huge organisations, often PLCs, and it would be impossible for one man to oversee everything including team affairs.

Quite where that leaves the clubs in the lower leagues is another matter entirely. If you venture further down to League One and League Two you'll still find clubs operating as one-man bands, where the manager is in charge of everything from the youth team to press enquiries but without the financial rewards that managers higher up the league structure receive.

In the past I would get upset with clubs and managers who wouldn't let one of their players come on *Soccer AM*, especially if they were injured or suspended and wouldn't be doing anything anyway. Today, though, I can understand entirely why they didn't want to help out. With so much on their plate, it is much easier for them to say no to requests like ours than say yes and then have to deal with another problem come Monday morning.

It's a difficult job for a football club to choose a manager. There is no correlation between being a great player and a great manager. Mourinho, Benitez, Wenger and Ferguson – all great managers, none of them world-class players. Thought it's always interesting when a former player becomes a manager because they have to make lots of important decisions as to what sort of gaffer they are going to be.

None more relevant than whether they wear a tracksuit or a suit in the technical area. A good example of this is Roy Keane, who was lucky enough to be managed by two of the greats of the game in Brian Clough (tracksuit manager) and Alex Ferguson (suited and booted). On his first match in charge of Sunderland I was keen to see which way he'd go, and the Fergie look won the day, making me feel this is the sort of manager he's chosen to be: tough, uncompromising, disciplined, potentially at war with the media as opposed to Cloughie, who loved courting the journalists and enjoyed the limelight.

The general rule of thumb: tracksuits means running up and down the sidelines, animated, gesticulating wildly, and celebrating goals by leaping up and punching the air. You're one of the boys, kicking every ball and fighting from the front. Think Martin O'Neil, Stuart Pearce. A suited manager gives the impression of the shrewd, wily tactician, the CEO managing a selection of expensive assets. They don't like to show their emotions as much, as everything that happens on the pitch they predicted anyway. Think Wenger, Sven and Benitez.

Tracksuits or suited, the following is some of my own experiences with managers up and down the years.

ALEX **FERGUSON**

Jesper Blomquist. Probably most Man Utd fans remember him as a bit-part player in their Treble season. However, in my time at *Soccer AM*, Blomquist was the only player that Alex Ferguson ever let me interview and that was because he was out of contract, still training with Man Utd, but really sat around doing nothing, waiting to go to Everton.

For years, Fergie's policy of never letting us do a thing with his players irritated the hell out of me. We never had any of them on the show, they never did the crossbar challenge and we couldn't even get a single phone interview with one of the team. Anything we ever asked for just got declined. It got to the stage where we phoned up their PR department every week just to put a request in, simply to try and annoy them. I lost count of the number of times I spoke to the players socially and they wanted to know why they could never come on the show and I had to explain to them that the boss wouldn't sanction it. It was only when I heard an interview with the goalkeeper Jim Leighton that my opinion started to change. He explained how when he was at Aberdeen, Fergie used to ram home the message that everybody hated them and by fostering that kind of mentality, he managed to create a unique team spirit. It was precisely the same way he was running Manchester United and even though it's not much good for those in the media, you have to respect him for it, not least because he's turned United into the most successful British team in recent years. What makes him all the more remarkable is that he keeps coming back, bigger and better than ever. Just when you think he's lost it, back he comes again to win even more trophies. And even though he's a pensioner, he hasn't mellowed in the slightest.

You still know that if you are a reporter and you ask a rubbish question he is going to lynch you. You've got to love him for that. Long may he continue to manage a Man Utd team that finishes runners-up to Chelsea.

GORDON STRACHAN

I've always adored Gordon Strachan. Every time you listened to him in an interview there was none of the usual nondescript nonsense you tend to get from most managers just an endless stream of classic, memorable quotes. So, faced with such an archive of great material we decided to do a 'What Gordon Strachan said . . .' item on *Soccer AM*.

They were so good, here's some of the classics for the book:

Reporter: Welcome to Southampton Football Club. Do you think you are the right man to turn things around?
Strachan: No. I was asked if I thought I was the right man for the job and I said, 'No, I think they should have got George Graham because I'm useless.'

Reporter: Is that your best start to a season?
Strachan: Well I've still got a job so it's far better than the Coventry one, that's for sure.

Reporter: Gordon, you must be delighted with that result?
Strachan: You're spot on! You can read me like a book.

Strachan: I've got more important things to think about. I've got a yogurt to finish by today, the expiry date is today. That can be my priority rather than Agustin Delgado.

Reporter: Bang, there goes your unbeaten run. Can you take it?
Strachan: No, I'm just going to crumble like a wreck. I'll go home, become an alcoholic and maybe jump off a bridge. Umm, I think I can take it, yeah.

Reporter: There's no negative vibes or negative feelings here?
Strachan: Apart from yourself, we're all quite positive round here. I'm going to whack you over the head with a big stick, down negative man, down.

Reporter: Where will Marian Pahars fit into the team line-up?
Strachan: Not telling you! It's a secret.

Reporter: You don't take losing lightly, do you Gordon?
Strachan: I don't take stupid comments lightly either.

Reporter: So, Gordon, in what areas do you think Middlesbrough were better than you today?
Strachan: What areas? Mainly that big green one out there . . .

It's a shame my book's not as funny as Gordon Strachan's quotes!

A while later, I met him just after he had resigned from Southampton. He said: 'I used to think you were insulting me, but now I've retired and I've watched the show, you weren't insulting me at all, you were embracing me.'

It was exactly what I wanted to hear. Here was a manager, a man, who knew exactly what we were trying to do on the show and realised that nobody was trying to ridicule him or stitch him up. 'But when you are a manager and you are under pressure whenever anybody says anything about you,' he added, 'you immediately assume that they are out to get you.' Not at *Soccer AM* we weren't. I just thought he was a brilliant man who we wanted to promote. And, for that matter, I still do.

IAN HOLLOWAY

When Gordon Strachan left the scene, there was a big hole and all the manager quotes reverted to clichéd blandness. Then up stepped Ian Holloway with one of the greatest post-match quotes of all time: 'To put it in gentleman's terms if you've been out for a night and you're looking for a young lady and you pull one, some weeks they're good looking and some weeks they're not the best. Our performance today would have been not the best looking bird but at least we got her in the taxi. She weren't the best looking lady we ended up taking home but she was very pleasant and very nice, so thanks very much, let's have a coffee.'

Ian Holloway is the undisputed king of the managers. He is just brilliant, a genuine entertainer. That's why his teams and his club's fans love him. He is also incredibly passionate about the game. We used to have a kick around on FA Cup Final after *Soccer AM* where we would get everyone who was still hanging around to play. Sometimes it would be 20-a-side, you know the kind of thing. One year, Ian stayed on and he couldn't help himself. As we were playing all we could hear was 'Tuck in! Tuck in!' or 'Stay on your feet!' or 'Get the tackle in!' That is what makes a great manager. They have this in-built reaction to a game where they simply can't help themselves. They have to get involved.

HARRY REDKNAPP

I genuinely think Harry Redknapp is underrated and maybe should have been considered for the England manager's job simply because he has the respect of pretty much everyone within the game. What he has done with the clubs he has worked at has been nothing short of miraculous. He took Portsmouth, hardly the most attractive or fashionable club, and turned them into an established Premiership team and competing for silverware. When he was manager of West Ham he kept them in the Premiership against the odds. Apart from Marco Boogers, he seems to pull quality players out of the hat. He knows how to build a team and he always gets his tactics right. All the big clubs are scared of playing Portsmouth, and don't be shocked if they get into Europe soon. He's certainly a better manager than a tipster. Whatever positions his clubs were in, he always made himself accessible and again was never scared of the media. So on *Soccer AM*, every derby day, we used to phone him up, chat for a couple of minutes about his teams, and then get to the important bit of talking about the day's racing. Harry always had a tip for us. These tips weren't any old tips – these tips were from people in the know. Thankfully his signings always worked out better than his tips. Thanks to Harry, I've helped send some bookie's kid to private school.

JOSE MOURINHO

Modern day managers are under unbelievable pressure these days and unless you're winning the league or you're an overachieving smaller club then you simply have to deliver. With that in mind, the last thing you need is one of your players going on TV and saying anything that would put any more pressure on you or jeopardise your position.

But when The Special One came along he was like a breath of fresh air. He was one of a new age of managers who decided to use the media as much as he could. It was almost like he was saying 'Yeah, you can do what you like.' He was so confident in his ability. When we wanted to do *Soccer AM*'s crossbar challenge at Chelsea's training ground he had no qualms about it. He just asked John Terry if he wanted to organise it and let everyone get on with it. He even joined in. The flip side of Jose, though, is that if you're a player who steps out of line then you won't play for him. That's the deal.

The magic of Mourinho is that he manages to deflect everything the media throws at his squad, making himself the centre of attention and leaving his players to get on with preparations for the next big game. Clearly, he has learned to embrace the media and that's why all the press hang on his every word. He gives them the ammunition and they get their story. Not every manager can carry it off but not only is he a very funny man but he's very fair too. If you treat him with respect you'll always be welcome. If you don't, expect to be banned.

The first time I met Jose was at a function for Chelsea Football Club. We were waiting in a room when the great man entered. He oozed charisma and the whole room stopped and stared at him. He spotted me over the other side and made his way across to have a chat. He shook my hand and said to me, 'We like your show. Me and the boys watch it every Saturday to get ready for the match. It's very funny, keep up the good work.' I was really made up that a foreign manager was embracing British football culture.

I say this because there's been two big disappointments with other foreign managers who I don't think have quite grasped our football culture. Gerard Houllier used to say we at *Soccer AM* didn't take football seriously enough and we were not allowed access to any of their players during his reign. But the most disappointed I've ever been was with Arsene Wenger. I think Arsene is a quality manager and I've never heard a bad word said against him, but during my time on *Soccer AM* we asked Arsenal to do the Crossbar Challenge hundreds of times. The club always said, 'Arsene says no.' However, if you go on the internet a French football TV show not only has the exact same the Crossbar Challenge segment, but the featured team is Arsenal and Arsene Wenger is talking through his players as they do the challenge. This really hurt that we'd been turned down so many times and yet French TV was allowed access. However I don't dislike Arsene; how could you dislike a man who creates such beautiful football as he does?

When Mourinho left Stamford Bridge I was in complete shellshock, like all Chelsea fans. Being a Chelsea fan is never simple. Just when you think everything's dreamy, the manager gets sacked. We've seen it all before, with Gullit and Vialli, and to say I was gutted was the understatement of the year. The man was great for the club, and was great for the Premiership. He was a revelation when he came over here, as he gave Fergie and Wenger a run for their money with his classic post-match interviews, and broke up Arsenal and Man Utd's total domination of English football. He dealt with the media with an arrogance and a swagger that made him a pleasure to watch, and because this is football, you know one day he'll come back to Stamford Bridge and beat us with his new team.

KEVIN **KEEGAN**

What a great man. When he was the manager of Newcastle United the first time around, it was so refreshing to see a team play in a way that was so at odds with what everybody else was doing. It was just attack, attack, attack. Every week, they just went for it. Keegan's attitude was simply if you are going to score goals then we'll just score more goals than you. Of course, it didn't quite pan out the way he wanted (and the 4–3 classic against Liverpool was proof of that) but for the time he was in charge Newcastle were certainly one of the most exciting teams to watch. Think about that team: Asprilla, Ginola, Shearer, Ferdinand, Beardsley. Now he's back there. It was a difficult start for him but he certainly turned things around. There's starting to be a sparkle again at St James's Park, and I for one hope he recreates the magic. Football needs managers like Kevin Keegan.

NEIL **WARNOCK**

Neil Warnock is a unique breed of manager – there's not many of his type left. Neil Warnock says exactly what Neil Warnock is thinking. If he thinks the ref's cheated, he says it. If he falls out with the oppo manager, he tells him. There is nothing guarded about what Neil Warnock says. He speaks his mind and suffers the consequences afterwards. He also used to speak to *Soccer AM* at the drop of a hat. He's just a lovely, straight-talking football man, devoted to the game and incredibly passionate about the teams he manages. Over the years, a lot of people have fallen out with him for one reason or another but nobody can say he doesn't care about football.

The way I see it there are two types of manager. There is the cool, calm, collected type who rarely gets animated (I believe England used to have one) and then there is the mad, demented lunatic who never sits down, prowling the touchline for the entire game and screaming himself hoarse. In other words, Neil Warnock. It was so nice to see him finally get promotion up to the Premiership with Sheffield United, even if it was for just one season, because he looked like he enjoyed every minute of being up there with the big boys. No one can say he didn't deserve a shot at being Premiership manager.

BARRY FRY

I can't finish this chapter without mentioning Barry Fry. The man is a pure entertainer. He's such a funny bloke and always up for a laugh. Can you believe he used to be in the Man Utd team as

George Best? He gave us more laughs on that show than any other manager.

Helen Chamberlain once said she wanted Barry Fry to be England manager. Now that I would have liked to have seen.

BEING A MANAGER IS EASY!

What I love about football fans is the idea that they know more than the managers. Clearly in my case this is true, but for 99.9% of the rest of the population this is complete rubbish. What amazed me the most about being a Chelsea fan was even after

Jose Mourinho had won the league, there were still Chelsea fans telling me where he was going wrong. Being a club manager is obviously quite a hard job because you can buy in players from other countries to build your squad, whereas being England manager is dead easy as you only have English players to choose from. Sorry Steve, but let's face it, we all roughly know the first XI so it's just a matter of keeping your fingers crossed there's no injuries and no awkward moments with divots.

By the way, the biggest change in the last decade in managers is what they're called . . . and I don't mean 'useless ****'. I mean, Steve McClaren is England coach, whereas Terry Venables was England manager. When did managers suddenly become coaches?

13

LOVEJOY'S ON HIS WAY TO WEMBLEY

(AND OTHER NOTABLE FOOTBALL STADIUMS)

As well as watching and talking about football, I have to say my biggest love is playing and my obsession with the game has given me the opportunity to play at many great stadiums over the years: Anfield, Old Trafford and Portman Road, to name but two. That's a joke, by the way.

But it was the old Wembley that was the business. What an amazing place? When they announced they were going to knock it down I was absolutely gutted. I just thought that it was the most remarkable stadium in the world bar none. Yes it was old and yes it was decrepit but it reeked of history. It was a special place. It was sacred. Nowhere in the world compares to it.

Every footballer in the world, professional and amateur, young and old, wants to play at Wembley. I was lucky enough to play at the old stadium on many occasions and I have to say that they were some of the greatest experiences of my life. Living so close to Wembley, I had been there on countless occasions (to watch England more than Chelsea). I even know all the short cuts to get out of the ground quickest. As regulars will know, the stadium was so big that if you took the inside lane on the stairs on the way out, it really could save you a few minutes. The first time I played there was before the 1998 Coca-Cola Cup Final between Chelsea and Middlesbrough. I was in the Chelsea team, captained by Damon Albarn from Blur. We also had Phil Daniels, Nigel Benn and Frank

Bruno on our side. It was the classic blend of silk and steel, if you like. We all got a bus to the ground when Damon had to pick the team. He told us he was going to play Nigel Benn and Frank Bruno at the back whether they liked it or not. Nigel got on the bus and Damon asked him where he played. 'Up front,' said Nigel. 'Fine,' said Damon, 'You're up front.'

Frank then got on the bus and Damon asked him as well. Frank replied 'Anywhere but at the back.' 'Fine,' said Damon, at which point Phil Daniels started laughing hysterically. Damon might be able to write No1 hit singles but his captaincy skills leave a lot be desired.

But what Damon's tactical u-turn did was give me the opportunity to really savour my first taste of playing at Wembley. Phil Daniels gave me some good advice that day. He said: 'If you play at the back with me you'll see much more of the ball because everyone gets giddy and wants to hurtle up front and try and score goals.' He was spot on. So there was just me and Phil Daniels at the back and I absolutely loved it.

As the game wore on, though, I decided to venture up front and went on a surging run up the wing before crossing the ball into the box. But as I kicked it, I skidded a bit and took a huge divot out of the Wembley turf. I was absolutely gutted. As the game carried on I ran off to get the clump of turf I'd dug up and then I trotted over and put it back in, just like a golfer would.

I met a new friend that day, a guy called Eddie Deedigan. After the game, he came up to me in the hospitality area and told me he'd seen the whole episode, 'That,' he said, 'is the funniest thing I have ever seen, a footballer putting their own divot back on the pitch.' 'But it's Wembley,' I said, 'and they're about to play the final. I just had to put the divot back.'

THE GREATEST GOAL I NEVER SCORED

The greatest goal I could have scored was at Wembley Stadium. I was playing in a charity game and I'd picked the ball up in the opposition half, moved it forward and then unleashed what I can only describe as a piledriver of a shot from way, way outside the box. I watched as the ball screamed towards the top corner but just as I was about to wheel away and celebrate the greatest goal the old stadium had ever seen, Jamie Theakston leapt up and at full stretch tipped it onto the crossbar and away to safety. I have since decided that Jamie Theakston is, in all probability, the greatest goalkeeper in the history of the game.

STADIUMS I HAVE (DIS)GRACED

Playing at Wembley every other week is all well and good but just like the England team, sometimes I have to take my talents around the country, just to satisfy the overwhelming public demand. Over the years I have played at Ipswich's Portman Road, the Valley, Upton Park, Derby's old Baseball Ground, Old Trafford, Highbury, Villa Park and the real home of football, Stamford Bridge. But playing in front of a full house at Anfield was just incredible. I was part of a celebrity side taking on a team of Liverpool Legends to help raise money for the Tsunami relief effort. As we lined up on the pitch the announcer went through all the Liverpool players and every one of them, without exception, received a rapturous reception. Then, when they ran through the celebrity team, they were getting smaller ripples of applause until it got to my name at which point a massive boo rang out across the ground. It was just a brilliant moment. I guess that was the closest I've been to feeling what it must be like to be a proper footballer or at least experience what Gary Neville feels like every time he plays at Anfield. What made it even more special was that this was a game to help raise money for one of the worst natural disasters in the history of the world and still the Liverpool fans couldn't help themselves when it came to me. Now that's respect and I love the Liverpool fans for it.

MY FAVOURITE
DRESSING ROOM

As well as the pitches, I'm lucky enough to go into the dressing rooms, which most of the public will never get to see. The dressing room at Anfield is my favourite. I know they'll be knocking it down soon but just being in there with the rich history of that place, and the ever-present smell of linament, is just about as good as it gets for a football fan. You go to Old Trafford or Stamford Bridge and the more modern stadiums and they all smell like your local leisure centre. They are clean, comfortable and a little too clinical for my liking. But when you go to Anfield, it still smells of all the greats that have graced that ground; Alan Kennedy, Ray Kennedy, Emlyn Hughes, Phil Thomson, Phil Neal, Jimmy Case, Kevin Keegan, Kenny Dalglish. The list just goes on. Just fantastic. When I walked past the 'This Is Anfield' sign on the way out to the pitch I was just about to touch it, as everybody else was, but then I decided I couldn't. I figured that as a Chelsea fan it wasn't my right do something that means so much to Liverpool. It was almost sacrilegious. It felt the same when I went to Jerusalem. I queued for ages to see the stone connected to Jesus but when I got there I found I couldn't touch it because I'm not at all religious. It just wasn't my place. Respect is a really important thing in football. There's no bigger insult than disrespecting a fellow fan's shirt and badge.

In fact, a football shirt means so much that it takes something special, something truly dramatic for a man to wear the shirt of another team. Well, that's my excuse and I'm sticking to it . . .

Let me explain. There I was, summoned to Wembley Stadium to play in a curtain raiser before the season's curtain raiser, the Charity Shield. Great I thought, a run out at the home of football. But when I got there I discovered I'd be playing in . . .

THE ARSENAL KIT.

This was the first I had heard of it. Suddenly, I had visions of all these stories appearing on the internet. You know the kind of thing, first he was a Watford fan, then he supported Chelsea, now he's an Arsenal fan and so on and so forth. I though Chelsea fans would never speak to me again. There would be chants of Judas as I walked up the Fulham Road. I had two options. Put the shirt on, play the game and then suffer the ignominy of being made out as a Gooner for the rest of my days or say thanks but no thanks and then do the unthinkable and walk out on Wembley. But that wasn't really an option, was it?

So, faced with the prospect of endless humiliation I hatched a plan. As everyone was getting ready I grabbed a nearby roll of gaffer tape, ripped off a bit and when nobody was looking furtively covered up the Arsenal badge on my shirt without anyone noticing. Job done. Or so I thought.

When we got out on to the pitch we had just finished our warm-up when we were called over for a team photograph. As I chatted to my team-mate Bradley Walsh, who's a rabid Gooner, he noticed that I had covered up the club badge and wasn't very happy. 'That's not very respectful Tim, is it?' he said sternly. 'Do you know how many people would swap places with you today? I think you should take the tape off!' The look on his face spoke volumes. I felt awful, so I relented and took the tape off. So with the badge now there for everyone to see, I, Tim Lovejoy, Chelsea supporter, had my picture taken wearing an Arsenal shirt. Great.

As soon as the cameras had stopped, Bradley turned to me and started p****ing himself. He didn't give a damn whether I covered up the badge or not. It was a proper stitch up. Bloody git.

It's happened since too. I got a game at Old Trafford and turned up to be told I had to wear a Manchester United shirt. Then I was pursued all around the ground by Mani from Primal Scream and his camera, warning me that he was going to expose me to the world as a Cockney Red. I have to say, though, again it was worth it because Old Trafford is such an amazing stadium to play in.

While I'm at it I may as well come clean about all the other kits I've had to play in as well. Knoxy, from the Badgers, is a Birmingham fan and was playing for the London Birmingham City Supporters' Club team and he had roped in Fenners to play for them too. They played at the bottom of my road in Chiswick so I said if they were ever short to give me a call. I was really happy the next Sunday morning when they called me and told me I was playing but when I turned up at the dressing room it dawned on me that we would be playing in an actual old Birmingham City kit that had been worn by the players. I ended up playing for them for a couple of seasons and I always wore the Paul Furlong shirt because at least he had also played for Chelsea and Watford. The oppo players used to always do a double-take when they saw me in a Birmingham kit. They used to say, 'Aren't you that bloke off telly who's always banging on about being a Chelsea fan?' I never really knew what to say as I was, in truth, committing the ultimate sin.

I'm not so precious about what shirt I play in these days. The way I see it is that I would much rather play football than watch it and If I get the chance to play at some amazing stadiums in return for wearing an Arsenal or a United kit then it's a small price to pay. Would I wear a Spurs kit though? Do you know what? I probably would if it meant I could turn out at White Hart Lane. But would I be happy about it? Of course I bloody wouldn't. On that point, though, I'm not sure I could ever wear an Argentina or a Germany shirt, even if it did mean playing at the Olympic Stadium or the Estadio Monumental. That would require a lot, and I mean a lot, of soul searching. These are England's biggest enemies in football terms (probably because we've also been involved in conflicts with both of them) and I would have to look deep inside myself to even contemplate it.

Actually, I've contemplated it. For a game of football? Of course I would...

A NEW WEMBLEY

Now we have the new Wembley Stadium and everyone says it looks incrdible and how lucky we are to have it. But when the build was dragging on and the costs were soaring it became very fashionable for everyone in the media and the public alike to slag the stadium off. It would have been easy for me to follow suit but I decided to throw my and *Soccer AM*'s support behind it. I am glad I did now because the new Wembley is an astonishing piece of engineering that's as good as any other stadium in the world. No longer do you have to worry about the stairs down. You can get an escalator. Lucky for me, my support was rewarded with a game there on its opening day with me and the Badgers. In true boys' own fashion, not only did I score (it wasn't the first goal, that went to Mark Bright) but we did win the tournament and I became the first captain to lift a trophy at the brand new Wembley Stadium. The following day, a picture of me playing there appeared in *The Independent* newspaper. It has to be one of the highlights of my stellar football career. I had made the sports pages of a national newspaper for playing football.

14

BLOODY FOREIGNERS ... I LOVE 'EM!

As a football fan you have to have an opinion on the game. However, the one that really worries me – and, for some reason, is never questioned – is that there are too many foreigners in our game. I saw a piece on TV recently that argued about the negative impact that too many foreign players were having on our national game. Maybe I'm missing the point but does nobody remember how awful our football was before we started to get more and more foreigners in the game? Does nobody recall how we used to struggle to qualify for major tournaments? English football was definitely not at the top of its game and there were lots of average players getting England caps.

There are a lot of people out there who preach the too many foreigners in our football cliché but what annoys me is that this type of line is not a million miles away from some kind of hysterical National Front speech back in the 1970s. Not only is it the lowest common denominator 'they've come over here and are taking all our jobs' diatribe yet again but it just perpetuates the myth that foreign footballers are really bad for the English game.

The fact of the matter is we now have better English players than we've had since the 1970 World Cup. We went through the 1980s and 1990s with the odd player here and there that were genuinely great like Peter Beardsley, Glenn Hoddle or Paul

Gascogine but looking back there were a lot of players doing a job which shouldn't be the case in a national team, especially England's. Look across our national team and the first choice XI and there isn't one player who wouldn't walk into any side in Europe. We no longer have players in team that are there to make up the numbers. All the England players are there on merit now. When have we ever been able to say that before?

And that's another point. You have people talking about the 'British game' as if we have one national side and not four. Scottish, Welsh or Northern Irish players have no bearing on the England team.

It is no coincidence that prior to the influx of foreign players we were never assured of our places in major tournaments. Even when we made it we never did well. We bombed at Euro 92, didn't qualify for the World Cup in 1994 and only qualified for Euro 96 because we were hosts. Then, as the foreign players began to arrive, England got better. Not only did we begin to qualify at a canter, but we no longer had to hope and pray that we could get past the first round. It was quarter-finals at the very least.

The problem we have is that we've never really had the right attitude. The Germans have this innate belief that they are going to win and it takes them very far. Even at the last World Cup, when people had written them off, they still got to the semi-finals. We're not like that. We still have a tendency to freeze and only ever seem to come out of our shells when we've had a man sent off and the odds are stacked against us. I'm not sure we've ever had the right manager but Capello could be the man.

One of the best things the football authorities ever did was to get rid of the law that restricted the number of foreign players you could play in your team. Looking back, it was a ridiculous piece of legislation anyway. You would have teams like Manchester United being forced to field a weakened team every week and players like Roy Keane being classed as 'foreign'. It was crazy and the net result, of course, was that the value of homegrown British players went through the roof, even though they were no better or worse than their cheaper continental counterparts.

When that law was repealed, it signalled a new start for the game in this country. Gone were the days of overly physical football and lumping it up front to target men and back came skill and flair, guile and trickery. After the barren years of the European ban, it was just what the game needed in England. Now, we have a league that is arguably the best in the world. We are blessed with a fabulous array of talent on show every week and many of the most skilful young English players, like Wayne Rooney and Joe Cole, are ones that have grown up watching and playing with foreign players.

At my club, the influence of foreign players on the English players has been staggering. Look at Dennis Wise. He was always a reliable performer for Chelsea but when the likes of Didier Deschamps and Ruud Gullit came along, he blossomed into an altogether better player. His touch was significantly better and he suddenly seemed to have more time on the ball. More recently, you can take the example of John Terry who has enjoyed the benefits of playing and training with two World Cup winning central defenders, Marcel Desailly and Frank Leboeuf, and developed into so much more than just a traditional English centre-half. Would he be England captain now if he hadn't played with such great players? I don't think so.

But there was one foreign player at Stamford Bridge that really set the benchmark for all other foreign players: Gianfranco Zola. When he turned up at Chelsea he managed to light up the club and the Premiership, and put paid to those doubters who thought foreign players only ever came to England when they wanted to eke out a few more quid at the end of their careers. He was, as we all know, incredibly gifted on the pitch but the way he conducted himself off it was exemplary. He was professional, dedicated and humble with it. That's why he is still held in such great regard not just at the Bridge but among all football fans in this country.

But it's happened all over the English game. Eric Cantona seemed to single-handedly lift first Leeds United and then Manchester United to league titles. Juninho, Emerson and Ravenelli helped transform Middlesbrough. Kinkladze became a cult hero at Man City as did Tony Yeboah at Leeds. Di Canio and Carbone worked wonders at Sheffield Wednesday and Jurgen Klinsman performed miracles at Tottenham but just because he left after a couple of seasons, Alan Sugar branded him a mercenary and the label stuck, not just with Klinsman but with all foreign players.

Foreign players still get far too much stick for my liking (they're only here for the money, they all cheat, they don't like the cold weather, they're stifling homegrown talent, etc etc). Tiny fragments of it may have some validity – after all, George Weah did turn out for Chelsea when he'd seen better days – but, for the most part, it is rubbish. What foreign players have helped to do is turn the Premiership into the most attractive, high-octane competition in world football. In fact, I defy anyone to look at the standard of the game at the end of the old First Division to the Premiership today and tell me that what we're seeing now isn't a million times better than what it used to be. And why is that? Because foreign players and managers have not only embraced our game but we have embraced their's too. And can I just remind everyone, in the last two years of the Champions League, not only have three out of the four semi-finalists been Premiership teams, but there was more Englishmen playing than any other nationality. Journalists can say what they want about our game, but these are the facts and I think they're pretty impressive.

WELCOME
TO ENGLAND!

One thing I have noticed in the years since foreign players started arriving in our game is the way the British players welcome them to the country. Whenever a new foreign recruit arrives, the club's initiation ceremony dictates that the team joker has to cut the trouser legs of their expensive suit just to show how wacky him and his new team-mates are. Another thing they have to do is to teach them some new English words or phrases. For example, the best way to say 'hello' is to say 'F**** off,' so that they then go around telling everyone to 'f**** off' much to the amusement of the rest of the team.

This was one of the greatest moments in *Soccer AM* history, when West Ham's Ivory Coast player Samassi Abou came on as a guest with his interpreter. On asking how his English was coming on and if he'd learnt any new words, Samassi Abou told us that he'd been told one of the best things to say was 'F*** off'. Cue red faces of embarrassment, looks of shock and horror as he'd sworn on live TV. However the greatest bit of this story was that it wasn't Julian Dicks or Ian Pearce who told him to do this, it was the suave, sophisticated David Ginola.

The hardest part of the foreign invasion is the pronunciation of their names for the football fan. Every season as a presenter I used to spend ages trying to learn the names so I didn't look stupid. It always reminded me of my nan, God rest her soul. She had an old person's attitude and wasn't the most PC of people. I remember every time Wimbledon came round she used to always say, if Martina Navratilova wants to play over here in our tournament she should change her name to something we can pronounce. This seems to be the policy of our footballers.

New foreign players will be given a new nickname that a) makes pronunciation of his difficult real name redundant, and (b) is as English as is possible. At Chelsea, Roberto Di Matteo became Robbie, Gianfranco Zola became Frank, Ricardo Carvalho is Ricky and Petr Cech is simply Pete. The only exception to this rule, however, is that I've heard that when a new player arrives from the Far East he will immediately be called 'Chopsticks' or 'Noodles'. So much for kicking racism out of football.

What is funny though is the pronunciation that some commentators, pundits and managers give to foreign players when they do arrive. When you've already heard of the players concerned and it's a fairly straightforward name (Vialli, Zola, Cantona etc) it's not a problem but when the lesser known players turn up everybody just starts making it up as they go along, but adding a Spanish or a French accent (or that weird clearing the throat kind of sound they make abroad) as they do it just to make it sound more plausible.

Looking back, there were about a million different versions of Juninho's name when he joined Middlesbrough and there was always a debate about whether it was Ruud Gullit or Ruud Hullit. More recently, Manchester United's Gabriel Heinze has been called everything from 'Heinz', as in the 57 varieties baked beans and ketchup company, to 'Eeeensay', which is just ludicrous. The best example, perhaps, was when the Sky Commentator Martin Tyler decided to look into the correct pronunciation of the Chelsea goalkeeper Ed de Goey's name. Ever since he had arrived in England, people had called him 'de Hoy', assuming that the 'G' was an 'H' sound, much like Ruud Hullit, sorry Gullit. Then, one day, Tyler started calling him Ed de Goey with a 'G' sound instead. It was like what the hell is going on here? I find it's always more entertaining when the players in question have potentially rude sounding names though. I used to like how Barry Davies wrestled with the name of the German striker Stefan Kuntz in Euro 96, settling on 'Koontz' so as not to offend anyone. Likewise the Portuguese keeper Quim, which is, apparently, pronounced 'Keem'. Yeah, right. But there are some players' names that you just can't change, no matter how much you try. Go on, have a go at Danny Shittu? No? How about Rafael Scheidt then? Or Dean Windass?

VIEW TO A sKILL

Another of the positive effects of the foreign invasion was the return of skills to our football. In the Seventies we had an abundance of skilful players like Rodney Marsh, George Best, Frank Worthington, Charlie Cooke, Stan Bowles, etc. But in the Eighties it was all hoofing the ball up the park, getting stuck in, all in the name of percentage football. As Frank McLintock once said, 'If Franz Beckenbauer played for Watford, he'd just get in the way.' Which is clearly one of the greatest quotes of all time and summed up a whole decade of long-ball football. But then came Ginola, Kinkladze, Di Canio, Bergkamp, etc and the skills came flooding back into the game. It was no longer about percentage, it was all about possession.

I feel duty bound here to mention Andrei Kanchelskis because (a) he was one of the best foreign imports that Britain has witnessed, and (b) he performed two of the most ridiculous pieces of showboating I have ever seen and am ever likely to see. The first was when he was playing Rangers and he was taking on a full back wide on the right. As the defender jockeyed him, Andrei jumped up into the air like some crazed Ninja, performed a 360-degree spin, before landing, dribbling the ball over the byline and then falling over. The second was during another game for Rangers when he picked up the ball just inside the opposition half. With time and space, he jumped two-footed on to the top of the ball, put his hand to forehead, and stood there like a ship's lookout and then dismounted. Both of them were completely pointless which, thinking about it, just made them better.

FOOTBALL BRAIN

Here's a myth. Certain footballers are seen as more knowledgable and well-informed, purely based on the fact that they were skilful on the pitch. Sadly there is no correlation to this, but we still keep believing it. Take, for instance, UEFA chief Michel Platini. As soon as he was appointed I thought, 'We're going to regret this,' because I'd heard some of the ludicrous things he'd said in the past. Just because he can hit an accurate thirty-yard pass with backspin does not mean he has knowledge of how to run our sport. Commenting on the 39th game, he said 'Soon in England you'll have no English president (chairman), you already have no English coach, you have no English players, and maybe you'll have no clubs playing in England. It's a joke.' Is this an intelligent comment?

And the other myth is that the foreign players are more sophisticated and intelligent. I think this comes from the fact that they can speak English as well as their native tongue. However, I have to tell you, I've been out on a few nights and seen some of Europe's finest as drunk as our players. There's not a lot of difference between young men around the world. They like fun, fun, and ladies.

GLOVE STORY

The other thing foreign players have given us is that it is now OK for English players to admit they're cold. Last season, Tottenham's Pascal Chimbonda even wore gloves for the game against Wigan in April! And it was possibly the hottest April day in the history of the planet!

Gloves is one thing but the first player I recall wearing gloves and even tights was our own John Barnes when he was at Liverpool. If it wasn't the gloves or his tights, it was his boots. Do you remember the white boots he used to wear? When I first saw him playing in those I thought he had started playing in slippers. I'd heard about Alan Ball playing in white boots in the 1970s but seeing John Barnes seemed so weird, so alien, but now you've got every single colour boot under the sun, thanks, I like to think, to pioneers like John Barnes.

Anyway it seemed so weird, watching players running around in gloves and I remember heated conversations about whether they were allowed to take throw-ins, or if that would be cheating. Brilliant. They're commonplace now, and I've even been known to wear them playing with the boys and no one even raises any eyebrow.

STICK **WITH** WHAT **YOU** KNOW

For all the nonsense written about the lack of English players in the Premiership, there doesn't seem to be quite as much debate about the role that the lack of English managers plays in the problem.

After all, look at the two teams that are most often accused of never fielding English players: Chelsea and Arsenal. At Stamford Bridge, we have Jose Mourinho, a Portuguese coach, who has brought in Carvalho, Morais, Hilario, Maniche and Ferreira. That, I'd guess, is more Portuguese players than have ever been in the rest of the Premiership combined. Across the capital at Arsenal, they have a French manager, Arsene Wenger, who has relied on a steady influx of French players to bolster his squad. More recently, Rafa Benitez, a Spaniard, has spent heavily bringing Spanish players to Anfield.

But think about it. Why is that any different to say Harry Redknapp or Neil Warnock, both English managers, relying on English players to form the basis of their teams. The answer, of course, is that it's not. Managers will go with what they are comfortable with and what they know. There was a survey in one of the tabloids recently which showed that 60 per cent of squads in the Premiership are now made up of foreign players while only 27 per cent of Serie A squads are non-Italian. Sounds a lot, doesn't it? Well no, not when you consider that every single one of the managers in Serie A are actually Italian. In that respect, it's not the foreign players in the Premiership that are restricting the chances of English players but actually the lack of English managers. Though one thing is for sure whenever a good English player comes along, they all want him and he usually becomes club captain. So why don't the loonies calling for the restriction, instead for a restriction on foreign managers? I ask you, what's the difference?

BOYS WILL BE BOYS

When we invented the Crossbar Challenge on *Soccer AM* (actually I say 'we' but Sheephead always reckons it was his idea), it wasn't the ball hitting the crossbar that made it such a good item, it was the players' banter in the background which we all loved watching. This is the great thing about team sports and which makes them so special. We would often have players on *Soccer AM* and their teammates would be texting us trying to stitch them up. I've met a lot of famous people over the last fifteen years, yet I don't think I've met a footballer who hasn't had his feet firmly on the ground. This is because it doesn't matter how big you become, you still have to go into the dressing room and get caned by your teammates. Can you imagine what stick Jason McAteer got after he did a Head & Shoulders advert, and can you imagine the stick players are getting when their WAGs are turning up in the papers? What's great about football is that it doesn't matter what league you're in or how rich you are, it seems the dressing room is still just a playground. There is no better example of this than the Galacticos at Real Madrid. When I did my film with David Beckham, he told me that at Real Madrid it was just like any other dressing room with the players caning each other all the time. One minute, Zidane, Ronaldo and Beckham would be having a water bottle fight the next Roberto Carlos would be wiping his snot on

Beckham's hair just to annoy him and Becks would retaliate by pinching his backside.

I asked Beckham what the Real Madrid dressing was like before a match and he said that the manager would come in, have a quick word with everyone to make sure they knew what he wanted from them and then leave them for half an hour to prepare themselves. Some players, he revealed, said a little prayer, others just sat in silence, composing themselves. Then the Brazilians in the squad all got together and played keepy-uppy. So I asked David whether he joined in. 'No,' he laughed. 'They won't let me. They say I'm English and I'm not good enough to play with them.'

Talking of Real, I was lucky enough to get out there quite a bit to watch them, as guests of either Steve McManaman or David Beckham and there were always loads of English fans on the flights out to Spain. But I was lucky enough to go where most fans can only dream of – the Real Madrid dressing room, taking in the full-length pictures of the players on their lockers and their framed shirts above them, probably with my mouth wide open. I've stood in the centre circle with Beckham, imagining what it must be like to play there. It made the hairs on the back of my neck stand up.

But the greatest thing was that after the game I got to go into the players' lounge, which is when I really started acting like a big kid. As I stood there, the players started arriving. There was Carlos, Zidane, Figo, Raul, Guti. It was one star after another. So I did what any professional, reputable broadcaster does in that situation: I got my phone out and started texting my friends. 'What are you up to? I'm just standing here with Zizou . . . ?

WHEN IN ROME...

If the stresses and strains of British football are getting to you I highly recommend a trip to the continent where you can watch a match without any care for the result. A few years ago I went to the Rome derby between Lazio and Roma at the Stadio Olimpico. It's the fans that make that game. On one hand you have the legion of ultras on the Curva Nord with the flares and the drums and who sing constantly throughout the entire game. On the other you have the suave, stylish types in the main stand. When I went I was surrounded by women in fur coats and jewellery, and chain-smoking men in shades who looked like they had stepped off the set of *The Godfather*. They were the kind of menacing figures who could have you killed at a moment's notice and you know what? I loved it.

What was brilliant about it was that Lazio went one nil up before Roma came back and scored in the last minute at which point the stadium erupted. The flares went off, the Lazio fans were trying to get to the Roma fans and a full-on riot ensued. It was insane but also bizarre because when you are witnessing that kind of incident in a foreign country it seems so surreal. If all this happened in England, my stress levels would be going through the roof, but out there I didn't give a damn.

It's also really good fun watching a game when you really don't mind who wins. Every match I've ever watched over here, even if I want to be neutral, always ends up with me supporting one of the teams. On the Continent, you really can just lose yourself in the game and relax.

ZZ TOPS

While we're talking about foreign footballers it's about time we addressed the age-old problem of who is the best player of all time. Now, if you're going to be a football fan, there are certain things you simply have to know. For instance, Pele is never called Pele, he is called 'The Great Pele'. And why? Because he is the greatest player of all time. Or is he? Well, not in my opinion. As far as I'm concerned that honour should go to Zinedine Zidane. I admit it is almost impossible to compare, not merely because these are players from entirely different eras but also because these days you get to see so much more footage of the best players and as such it's easier to mount an argument in favour of them. But I do believe that in years to come people will be talking of Zinedine Zidane in the same breath as Pele and Maradona in the debate about the greatest player ever.

Let's face it, the man has everything in his locker: strength, pace, vision, goals, skill, the lot. David Beckham and Steve MacManaman have both said that they have never seen a man with such control over the football. Unlike Pele or Maradona, Zidane was a big man but that just made him a better player in that it gave him great ability in the air and the strength to make and ride tackles too. Moreover, Zizou has proved beyond any doubt that he could score goals at every level. He scored two in the 1998 World Cup Final against Brazil, scored a cracker of a winner in the Champions League Final in 2002 and has scored countless great goals for both Juve and Real Madrid at club level.

What was telling was that when he was in his prime, France

became the first team since Germany in 1974 to hold both the World Cup and the European Championship titles and even deposed Brazil as the number one ranked team in the world. In 2002, though, he missed the first two games of the World Cup with a thigh injury, came back too early and France, the reigning champions, went out in the first round. Later, having retired from international football, he came back to help France out of their qualifying mess for the 2006 World Cup and they not only won their group but went all the way to the final again. Even then, when he got sent off for head-butting Italy's Materazzi, he returned a hero, purely because he was protecting his mother's honour. That is a legend. That is an icon.

I have always said that to win a World Cup you need to have a truly exceptional player in your team and France certainly had that with Zinedine Zidane.

MY FAVOURITE
EVER PLAYER (IN THEORY)

Much as I admire and respect Zinedine Zidane, I must admit that my favourite player of all time is probably Johan Cruyff. But, this is a little weird. As a kid I watched some footage of him playing for Holland, it was only short, and the ball seemed to be almost glued to his foot. He was elegant, graceful and absolutely deadly. In fact, he is the sole reason that I always had to wear the number 14 shirt when I play. Whereas every other great player wore 7, 9 or 10, Cruyff wore a squad number on his back. I thought it was so different and so continental. As for the Cruyff turn, I spent hour after hour practising it until I could do it off my left foot and my right and now it's my signature trick. If truth be known it's my only trick and I'll still do it now, given half a chance. As I've seen so little of his footage, I think the mystique of the man has been built up in my mind and I have turned him into this iconic figure for me.

Like Maradona, Johan Cruyff had that rebellious streak about him. At the 1974 World Cup, for example, he tore one of the three Adidas stripes off his Dutch shirt because he had a deal with Puma. Then, four years later, he helped the Netherlands qualify for the finals in Argentina but refused to play in the tournament itself because it was a country under military rule where all manner of human rights abuses were being perpetrated by the ruling junta. That's why I loved Johan Cruyff. He was a rebel with a cause but with the skill, elegance and charisma to back it all up.

15

ONCE
UPON A TIME
IN
AMERICA

Unless you've been living under a large rock, or maybe in Grimsby for the past year, you may well have noticed that England's most famous footballer, David Beckham, now plays for the Los Angeles Galaxy in America's Major League Soccer (MLS).

It's a brave move by Beckham. After all, they've tried to break football before in the US and failed. Back in the 1970s, for example, Pele came out of retirement to play for the New York Cosmos in the North American Soccer League (NASL). Money flooded the game. Other stars like Franz Beckenbauer and Johan Cruyff, Gerd Muller and Bobby Moore went over to try their luck but, despite their best efforts, even they couldn't sell soccer to the States. Will Beckham fare any better? It's too early to tell. But if there's one player in the world who might just help convince America that 'soccer' is the greatest game of all, then it has got to be Becks.

Soccer. I don't even really like the word. In fact, when I got the job on *Soccer AM* one of the first things I tried to do was to get the name changed. I wanted the show to be called *Football AM* because that was what we played in this country. That was British. Soccer was that game that mums took their kids to play across the pond. Believe me, I had the letters of complaint from the viewers to back me up too. But I didn't get my way. The powers that be at

Sky put their foot down and told me that was how it was going to be and, looking back, I'm glad we stuck with it.

I love football all over the world and America is the last place that hasn't truly embraced it and made it into its No. 1 sport. I don't think this will ever happen, but I do think it will grow significantly. The show I did on Channel Five wasn't a major success over here, but we got people watching it on the internet from all over the world, especially America, but also Japan and even Russia. The MLS has really caught the imagination of football fans around the world. Many people have said that David Beckham hasn't made an impact but this just isn't true. When he scored his first goal, over a million people downloaded it on YouTube the next day. Since he's been playing merchandise sales have gone up 700% for the LA Galaxy and 300% league-wide. Adidas have made 600,000 Beckham shirts to cope with the demand, and Herbalife, the shirt sponsors, believe they'd achieved 900 million media impressions in the two weeks around when Beckham and the new team's shirts were first introduced. This is all pretty impressive from just one signing. He might not be the best player in the world, but he's certainly the biggest. To be honest, when I worked on the MLS it was a refreshing change not just because it's a different programme but because it gave me a new insight into just how the game can be covered. Don't get me wrong, MLS has its faults. Sometimes you'll be watching the footage thinking 'this is absolutely out of this world'. Other times, you'll be watching it with your head in your hands thinking, 'blimey, this is bloody awful'.

The commonly held assumption in the UK is that the standard of MLS is like that of the Championship in England, but I don't see it myself. The problem with MLS is the sheer range of players playing in the competition. On one hand you have players who would struggle to get into a Championship side; on the other you have players that wouldn't look out of place in the Premiership. Yes, the games and the quality may be a bit random at the moment and it may well take a good couple of years for it to settle down, but that is all part of the appeal.

But just as they can learn a lot from us in terms of how to play the game, we too can learn a lot more about how we cover football. In that respect, it's a mutually beneficial deal. Across the world football is pretty much played and televised in the same way, but in America, where sports like basketball, baseball and gridiron rule the roost, they are doing it in their own inimitable way. On the live games, for example, they allow journalists in the locker room and even interview the players and coaches during the game and as they're walking off at half-time. I know that in the Champions League you may see a brief interview with the manager before the start of the second half but you never get a sniff of the players, let alone get to go in the locker room, unless you're watching Sentana's Conference coverage. I saw one clip from MLS recently where the keeper had saved two PKs (that's penalty-kicks in American) in the first half and when he had finished his pitchside interview he just turned to the camera and said: 'I'd like to thank you for watching at home.' I just loved this stuff. I've also watched games recently where they get the players on the bench to shuffle up and they start interviewing the substitutes right in the middle of the game. They even rang up the LA Galaxy's former coach, Frank Yallop, during a match just to have a chat about David Beckham. You can ridicule it all you like, but it gives you an insight you just don't get in our football.

Everything is different in MLS. When you win the league in the

UK, for example, you get a medal in recognition of your achievement. If you and your team win the MLS, though, you get a ring. That's class. A nice big sov (takes me back to my casual days). In fact, maybe we should follow suit. Mind you, if we did dish out rings instead of medals over here, you'd have players like Ryan Giggs walking round looking like Jimmy Saville.

There's also a whole new language to learn when you're watching the American game. I've already mentioned penalty kicks being 'PKs' but there's a host of their classics that we'll all soon be using in this country. Or maybe not. But they're fun anyway. The halfway line? That's the 'midfield stripe'. The league table? That's the 'league ladder'. If you've lost your last three games, you're 'zero from three'. And matches, lest you forget, are never drawn, they are 'tied'. My favourite, though, has to be the name they give to a goal scored away from home. Now, whenever someone scores on their travels in the MLS, it's chalked up as a 'road goal'. Here's some more:

SLOW ROLLER. A term used to describe a weak shot.

WASTE BASKET. A phrase often used to describe a pass that goes out of play.

REAL ESTATE. Used to describe the space/lack of space in the penalty area.

MATCH UPS. Term used to describe man-marking.

On the diagonal Service. The term used to describe a cross field pass.

Showing the foot skill. A phrase used to highlight good skill from a player.

Southpaw. A phrase adopted from the boxing term for a left handed fighter. Used to describe a left footed player.

UNLOADS. The phrase used to describe when a player kicks a ball with maximum effort.

ON FRAME. The term used to describe when a shot was on target.

IN THE WHEEL HOUSE. The phrase used to describe the area within easy reach of a keeper. English alternative, 'down the keeper's throat'.

UNCORK IT. The phrase used to describe the unleashing of a powerful shot.

SOME WHEELS. The term used to describe when a player shows a quick turn of pace.

CHICKEN WING BATTLE. The phrase used to describe a tussle between players, in which there is excessive use of arms and elbows.

BULLDOGGING. The phrase used to describe when a player shows determination to win the ball back.

KNOCK LIKE A BEAR KISS. The phrase used to describe when a tackle is more clumsy than dangerous, and appears to be worse than it actually was.

'. . . right on **THE DOORSTEP**'

THE DOORSTEP. The term used to describe when a player is in front of goal.

'. . . with the **ONE TOUCH**.'

ONE TOUCH. The phrase used to describe when a player passes or shoots fist time, without taking an extra touch.

'. . . with the **TAKEAWAY**.'

TAKEAWAY. The term used to describe when a player makes an interception or tackle, and comes away with the ball.

'. . . there's the **FINAL SIGNAL**.'

FINAL SIGNAL. The term used to describe when the referee blows for full time. English alternative, 'Final Whistle.'

'. . . with the **STUTTER STEP**.'

STUTTER STEP. The phrase used to describe when a player uses a dummy to deceive an opponent.

'. . . oh, nice **RIP**.'

RIP. The term used to describe when a player produces a well hit shot.

'. . . **TOP OF THE D**.'

TOP OF THE D. The phrase used to describe the edge of the box.

'. . . they are a **GREAT ROAD TEAM**.'

GREAT ROAD TEAM. The phrase used to describe a team who is successful away from home.

Even the commentators don't have real names. They're called PJ or Max, not Martin or Andy, Barry or John. It's just like the 'Boston Goals' feature we used to do every week on *Soccer AM* but better. But it's on the stats side that they really go overboard and if you thought Jonathan Pearce was bad then wait till you watch Major League Soccer. It's a proper stats fest and where they lead, we will inevitably follow. It's like the clock and the score you see in the corner of the screen during live matches. When Sky started doing that a lot of people were very sceptical. It was like 'Why have they got the score in the corner of the screen? We all know what the bloody score is!' But it was great when you came in half way through a live match and the score was up there in the corner of the screen. So where did you think we stole that idea from? That's right, the States. Yes, it's a blindingly obvious concept but nobody thought of it here, did they?

I was working at Sky Sports when the stats explosion started to happen in the British game. Suddenly, there was all these crazy graphics and whooshing noises going off all the time. Now we were doing possession stats and people were like 'Possession? Who gives a damn about possession?' when, in fact, it's one of the biggest indicators of how a match is going. When it first happened it seemed alien, but now it's part and parcel of the televised game. It's this detail that American sports fans love and I'm sure you'll soon be seeing some of the other innovations that MLS is using. Recently, there was a game when one team were awarded a penalty and before the kick was taken they quickly showed the footage of the last four penalties the player had taken, showing exactly where he intended to place his shots. You know, that's not rocket science. All it takes is a bit of pre-match preparation, a bit of research, and you have a really interesting angle.

I can see that catching on in the Premiership. With every kick in the league now covered, you could quite easily do it here, not just for penalties but for free-kicks outside the box or even the way a particular player takes his corner kicks. There was some footage of the former Aston Villa striker Juan Pablo Angel playing for Red

Bull New York recently and scoring a penalty. Before he took the spot kick, they rolled out all these statistics about his penalty record in the Premiership and the likelihood of him scoring. These are the stats we want not the John Motson ones about it being 57 years since Blackburn Rovers last played Fulham on a Monday night wearing blue and who's got the lucky end.

Let's get the proper stats. We want to know where a player put his last ten penalties. We want to know what he's thinking. After all, if goalkeepers can do their homework and look into the penalty-taking habits of their next opponents why can't the television companies over here do it? In America, where their sports are inundated with facts and figures, statistics and analysis, it's the first thing they think of because it's what their audience demand. We're different in the UK. We don't like change. Remember when they tampered with the theme tune to *Match of the Day*? There were nearly riots on the streets of Britain. I'm not like that. I embrace change, I like new and interesting ways of looking at things and that's what MLS is going to give us.

Besides, it can work over here. Look at cricket. In the last 20 years, the coverage has changed beyond belief. Today, the analysis is phenomenal, the graphics are truly innovative and the research extremely thorough. Slowly, it is creeping into football too. Thanks to Sky, the analysis of the game over here is becoming increasingly Americanised. It took a long time but features like the tactics board, the on-screen scoreboard and even the replay whoosh, are quintessentially American innovations that have now found favour in the UK to the point where you can't actually imagine watching a game on Sky without them. We have even got to the stage now where we have split screen football on Champions League coverage, which is absolutely brilliant. I have sat there and watched eight screens of football in one go, flicking between them. It's like Robbie Williams walking into a room full of girls. Take your pick, fill your boots, tuck in.

That's why we should embrace America and the MLS because regardless of what you think of the standard of football on offer, it will inevitably have knock-on effects on the game throughout the world. I, for one, hope the game finally takes off in the States and if it could make a dent in the dominance of basketball, baseball, ice hockey and so on it would be amazing. What gives me hope for the American game is not just that they seemed to have learned the lessons from the spend, spend, spend culture of the NASL but that 30 years after Pele called it a day at the Cosmos, the world is also a much smaller place. Through the internet we'll all be able to check out what's been happening in MLS at the click of a mouse. It won't just be that game on the other side of the Atlantic.

Of course, we all know that Asia, Africa, South America and, obviously, Europe embrace football and that it is the national game in virtually every country. The United States and Canada, meanwhile, remain the only two major territories where the game has yet to get a real foothold. What will help with the conversion process is that you've got so many Spanish, Italians, Mexicans, Greeks and South American immigrants living in the United States. These, after all, are nations with a rich heritage when it comes to football. These are people that know and understand the game and that need their regular fix of football. That, coupled with 20 million (and rising) registered young players in the States, should give the game a half decent chance of prospering.

What's more, the United States now has an international team that is no longer a laughing stock. Slowly, they are becoming a force. They qualify regularly for the World Cup and, much like Australia, they play with passion and no small amount of flair. If they can just learn some of the discipline, some of the percentage play, of teams like Germany then there's no reason why they can't do really well in a World Cup sooner rather than later. Whatever happens, I'm convinced that it's going to be entertaining. We're seeing some famous footballers go over there such as Abel Xavier and Juan Pablo Angel and now David Beckham, who has pledged his allegiance to the cause. There's even rumours that Zinedine Zidane was tempted to come out of retirement to try his hand in the land of the free. Now that would have been interesting.

However what they need more than anything in the MLS is to appoint some decent managers who can bring some tactical discipline. Gullit is now the manager of LA Galaxy, which will give it more credibility, the football will soon start improving and the league will soon take shape.

For any of you doubting whether there's enough interest to sustain the game in the States, I'll leave you with one statistic. There are more people playing football in the US than there are in England, Germany, Brazil and Argentina combined. Fact.

16

THERE'LL ALWAYS BE AN ENGLAND

When I was a kid England was everything. England was where it was all at. It was Kevin Keegan and Trevor Brooking, Ray Wilkins and Bryan Robson. The first ever game I went to was an England game, can you believe? Not Chelsea or Watford, but England. A mate's dad took me to Wembley to see Ron Greenwood's England and I couldn't understand why England, my England, were getting booed by their own fans. As they read the team out over the public address system, Keegan and Brooking would get massive cheers and then some of the other players would get booed. It made no sense. I always thought you were meant to boo the opposition, in fact that was pretty much expected, but to boo your own players? I was horrified. Now, of course, it's almost mandatory to boo the England team.

The thing about that England game is that I can't even remember who they were playing. All I know is that they were a team in red. Was it Poland? Norway maybe? Perhaps it was Spain. I just don't know. But then I can never remember anything about football matches, as you know. I'm not alone. I heard that Michael Ballack has no recollection of his first Champions' League match or the time he scored against Real Madrid. Doesn't have the foggiest. I'm like that. I can't even remember the first Chelsea game I went to. You can say what you want about supporting

England (and most people do) but it is never a dull experience. We always make it to the finals, always get to the quarter or semis and then, obviously, always get knocked out on penalties. The thing that keeps every England fan going is the fact that before we get eliminated we always show some promise, always threaten to finally do something; the 5–1 win over Germany, the demolition of Holland in 1996, the victory over Argentina in 2002, that mind blowing Michael Owen goal against the same opponents in 1998. Mind you, we lost that on penalties, didn't we?

But there have been some incredible highs and some all too depressing lows following England. When I was a kid, England had a rough time of it, especially in the 1970s. That was the decade when Scotland seemed to qualify for everything and England never did. Things have changed since then but we still have the same mindset, the same sense that we'll never quite make that final leap.

The trouble is that I actually think we like losing. It's the Manchester City syndrome; the lower down the leagues they slide the more fans they seem to get. It's the same with England. The worse we are, the more people like them. Think about it. When have you ever been to the pub to watch an England game and someone has said: 'I really fancy England tonight, we're going all the way'. They don't, do they? No, when you go to the pub, someone will say 'I've got a bad feeling about this game' and it'll just be a stroll against San Marino or Andorra. When, exactly, did we start worrying about the easiest of matches? Also, why is it that before every tournament, we start believing we're overrated? That's nonsense. You put our squad up against any other in the world and, on paper, they're every bit as good any other out there. Unfortunately, football is played on grass.

It's a negative attitude that has to change and I think if we are going to win the World Cup again we have got to turn into Germans. That means believing that we are the best team around, believing that we can dominate the opposition and believing that we can, and will, win the World Cup. And eating sauerkraut. Look at the attitude of the then German national manager Rudi Voller in the run-up to the 2002 World Cup. In an interview just before the tournament started, he said, 'Everyone thinks Holland are a better team than Germany, but I bet we do better than them.' Holland hadn't qualified. He went on to say, 'Tournament football's different. We're in it, so we might as well win it.' He took a mediocre team all the way to the final and narrowly lost to Brazil. You see once you are in a tournament it is irrelevant what your form in the qualifiers was like. It's a clean slate and you've just got to get on and win it. We, and by that I mean the England team, always seem to have the weight of the world on our shoulders. How can we change things? We all need to get behind England and be positive . . .

SHOOT!

I love football more these days than I ever have done, but one thing I miss is that back in the 1970s and 1980s, whenever England played abroad there would always be a promotional photo-shoot wherein a couple of the players would either dress up in the local costume or be pictured pretending to eat the local

This is a collector's item – a penalty I actually scored!

The first-ever Badgers line-up. We went on to beat Rutland Rovers.

This is when the Badgers went big-time and introduced ex-pros Phil Neal, John Wark, Mickey Thomas and Alan Kennedy.

Me training at Torquay. I thought wearing golden boots was a good idea until I saw the look on their faces when I put them on in the dressing room. Needless to say, I got the punishment I deserved.

Me pictured with Guti on one of my many trips to Madrid. I got a lot of stick after putting this on *Soccer AM*.

Paul Gardner - the real Chip - with wife Sarah.

A very early script meeting. I know I've got big sideburns but I promise it wasn't in the 70s.

Soccer AM chaos. Martin O'Neil, Fergie, the Zookeeper and Fenners dancing to 'Happy Hour' by the Housemartins. How we stayed on air for ten years with that rubbish God only knows.

'This is proof that I did actually get to hold the World Cup.

Soccer AM celebrating fifty episodes under my leadership. We went on to make over 450 episodes under my reign.

As you can tell, I hated doing publicity shots.

Certificate No. 5608   No. of Shares ...1....

CHELSEA PITCH OWNERS
PLC

This is to Certify that .....Tim Lovejoy.....................

of ....

is the registered holder of .....1..... Share(s) of
£100 each fully paid in the above named Company,
subject to the Memorandum and Articles of
Association of the Company.

The Common Seal of the Company was hereto affixed in
the presence of:

Authorised Signatory

Registration Date

No Transfer of any of the above Share(s) can be
registered unless accompanied by this Certificate.

Proof I own part of the Chelsea pitch and my first step on the way to
becoming the new Roman Abramovich.

delicacy. Tricky qualifier in Norway? Let's dress Mark Hateley and Terry Fenwick up as vikings. Friendly in Italy? Give Terry Butcher a pizza to pose with. Pressure game in Spain? Get Steve Hodge a matador's outfit.

Sadly, now whenever England play away all you get is a stage-managed press conference where the management pick on one player to come out and face the hacks. That's not half as much fun. One day, maybe one glorious day, they'll get Rio Ferdinand in lederhosen for that must-win match in Munich.

BRING BACK THE DENTIST'S CHAIR

Do you remember England's brief tour to China and Hong Kong in the lead up to Euro 96? Of course you don't but then nor do I. Perhaps the only thing you may recall about that trip, in fact, is the furore over the so-called 'Dentist's Chair'. The England team had gone out to celebrate Gazza's birthday and ended up shooting shots of vodka, tequila and whatever they could lay their hands on down Teddy Sheringham's neck. At the time, the condemnation in the press was typically over the top. They were a disgrace, they weren't fit to wear the Three Lions, blah, blah, blah...

But think about it. What was the upshot? I'll tell you. We went and had one of our best ever tournaments at Euro 96, thrashing Holland along the way and very nearly getting to the final. On that basis, I think the Dentist's Chair should be a compulsory part of any England get-together, especially before a major championship. The way I see it, the whole episode created a camaraderie and a togetherness that no amount of sports psychologists or motivational speakers could ever achieve. In fact, Steve McLaren should think very seriously about re-introducing it.

An interesting postcript to this is that Teddy Sheringham, the man in the Dentist's Chair, is still playing football for Colchester United at the age of 41. Maybe tequila is the secret of eternal youth?

THE PROBLEM
WITH ENGLAND SONGS

I blame Baddiel and Skinner. If it wasn't for them and their admittedly brilliant 'Three Lions' we'd still have England World Cup songs that actually featured the players. Now, whenever a major championship comes around, every Tom, Dick and Harry in the known world thinks they can write an England song. At the last World Cup, for example, we got sent about seventy-five songs from people wanting *Soccer AM* to get behind their 'unofficial England anthem' but how can you when they are all, without fail, unbelievably crap?

Worse still, it's now started a trend where there's now an official England song that doesn't actually feature any of the players either. Ant and Dec, Embrace, Echo and the Bunnymen, with the Spice Girls, they've all had a go since Euro 96. They hype up these tunes with loads of PR and expensively-produced videos…and none of the players get involved. It's all Ant doing keepy-uppies or Ginger Spice scoring a half-volley. Which is just plain wrong. We want the John Barnes rap. We demand vocals from JT and Wayne Rooney. And Steve McClaren should be forced to dance on top of the bar.

WHY WHITE?

For all the rubbish written about the England team in recent years – and there have been a lot – there has never really been one conclusive argument mounted to suggest exactly why they've failed to repeat the success of 1966. Until now, that is. I truly believe that the reason England has failed to match those heady days of Moore, Charlton, Peters and Hurst is because we play in white. You see, white is a passive colour (I discuss this later in the book) and the day we actually won the World Cup England was wearing red while the Germans were wearing? Yes, you at the back? Correct, white. With that in mind, I think it's about time we changed the England kit so that red is the first choice colour of the national team. Then and only then will England be able to begin their ascent back to the summit of world football. And while we're on the subject, why is there blue in the England kit when our flag is red and white?

SING **YOUR** HEARTS OUT

Whether you're a royalist or not, I think it should be compulsory for players to sing the national anthem. 'God Save The Queen' is our answer to the All Black's 'haka'. There is nothing better for England fans than to see the players belting out the national anthem. It makes you proud to support your national team. It can't be that hard to learn the words. And even it is, surely Sir Trevor Brooking can print out lyric sheets so the squad can learn it in the team hotel.

COME TOGETHER

The great thing about supporting England is that it gives supporters of smaller clubs a taste of the big time. While followers of Arsenal, Man Utd, Liverpool and Chelsea are too spoilt by the vast number of big games they play in the world's greatest stadia, those of you who support, say, Hull City or Darlington will never get the slightest sniff. That's why I always laugh when you see all the England flags at international games with 'Stevenage' or 'Halifax' on them.

It's also amazing to see how people's attitudes to players change when they put on an England shirt. It's like David Beckham. As you know, I openly admit I wasn't his biggest fan back in the day – and I told him that to his face when I made my documentary with him – but as soon he was playing for England one was his number one fan. You'll have die-hard Evertonians who suddenly become Stevie G's greatest admirers, or City fans cheering on Rio Ferdinand. That's why the national team will always be so important because it's the one time fans of every club can come together for a common cause.

MANAGING
EXPECTATIONS

It's often said that the job of England manager is more difficult than that of Prime Minister. That, of course, is rubbish. I mean, it's not like Kevin Keegan ever declared war on anyone or as if Graham Taylor had to commit billions of taxpayers' money to a nuclear defence system, is it?

OK, so it can be a tough job but that's only because the media, or rather the tabloids, will have it in for you from day one. The truth is that if you're England manager you are damned if you do and damned if you don't, so the tendency is for them to play it safe rather than pick the luxury or flair players. That's why Glenn Hoddle never got a sustained run in the England side. Everybody else in the world knew he was the most gifted player we possessed yet we went with Bryan Robson, a great, great player and maybe more versatile than Hoddle who needed to be in the middle of the pitch.

It was the same with Matt Le Tissier. Here was a player who single-handedly kept Southampton in the Premier League year after year, never missed a penalty and who scored the kind of goals that beggared belief. But I've checked and he only won eight caps for England when he should have won 50. Ironically, when he scored a hat-trick for England B against Russia in 1998 it looked like he had booked his place in the World Cup squad but it was the then manager, Glenn Hoddle, who chose not to take him.

We still suffer from the same percentage football mentality today. We now have a good England side and one that could go on to great things but there is still that overriding sense that we continue to pick players and systems who won't lose us matches rather than the ones who might just win them for us. Is that the fault of the England manager? I don't think so. If anything, it's the fault of the media.

These days, you need a big, big personality to be the England manager. Initially, Sven-Goran Eriksson seemed to cope really well with the pressures of the job. Maybe because he was foreign we seemed to give him a little more leeway than his predecessors and maybe because he was new to the country he wasn't as familiar with the whole media circus that surrounds the position. For a while, all parties seemed to be happy with the arrangement but when it went wrong the backlash was just as savage, if not more so, than it had been for Graham Taylor.

Perhaps the only England manager in recent memory to handle the job with any kind of success was Terry Venables. Not only did he have a rapport with the media but he had the respect of all his players. Having spoken to some of the players from that era, there was respect on both sides. He gave them a bit of freedom, let them go for a drink and so on, and in return they gave him their all.

We now have Fabio Capello as England manager, and I think he is the man to take us all the way. We're going to win the World Cup! ow bloomin' excited am I that finally I feel we've made the right decision? I thought we should've gone for Capello or Marcello Lippi after Sven-Goran Eriksson left so although it's a little late, at least we have our man.

Now the important thing is for us all to leave him alone. If the FA think he's good enough for the job, he needs 100% complete control. He should be allowed to choose everything from his team to his captain to his own staff to whether the pitch is watered before, during and after games.

I imagine that sometimes the football might not be pretty under Capello, but if we really do want to go far as a nation we need to be patient because the man is a born winner.

This is a man who had no qualms in dropping David Beckham from the Real Madrid team. He had the balls to do it even though David's a player that sells more shirts than anyone else in the world. And what's great about him is he had even bigger balls to bring him back into the team when he realised he needed to use him. (Ha! I've just realised this sounds a bit like Steve McClaren!).

When we won the World Cup under Sir Alf Ramsay, apparently it was all about building a strong team, not individuals and I think Capello won't be any different. Even the so-called definite starters like Wayne Rooney must be a little worried about their places which I think can only be a good thing.

Imagine being an England player in the dressing room and looking up and seeing Capello walking around - surely that must be enough to inspire you onto victory?

As a nation we are paying him top Euros so why don't we just get behind him, support him, have trust and faith and hopefully, he'll bring silverware back to good old Blighty. Can you imagine the feeling of us winning the World Cup? I haven't been this excited about a managerial appointment in years. I really do think the FA have got it right.

17

WHY NOTHING BEATS PLAYING FOOTBALL

Time: 0230 hours
Date: February 18th, 2007
Location: My bed, London . . .

It had taken a long time but finally I had been spotted. And not just spotted by some lower league team or semi-pro outfit, but by my team, my life, Chelsea. With the contracts signed and the press conference conducted I meet my new team-mates. JT takes me round the dressing room, Frank Lampard grins and shakes my hand, Joey Cole pats me on the back. Ballack nods, Shevchenko smiles. This is it.

Match day. An FA Cup tie against Leeds. Jose Mourinho runs through his team talk. Keep it tight. We're better than these. Don't let up. We huddle and head to the pitch. I take my place on the bench, shuffling in between Shaun Wright-Phillips and Arjen Robben. The game starts. Twenty five minutes in and Didier Drogba gets on the end of a Joe Cole cross. One nil.

The second half. We're coasting. Then Claude Makalele goes down after a hefty challenge. He's hurt. Mourinho gives me the nod. I strip off my tracksuit and warm up. The physio signals to the bench that Makalele can't carry on. This is it.

I'm going on. The boss pulls me in and explains what he wants me to do. Sit in front of the back four. Break up their attacks. Let nothing through. I shake hands with the hobbling Makalele. This is it.

Twenty minutes of midfield shuttles, I was breaking down attacks winning the ball and laying it off just like the gaffa had asked. All that fitness training had paid off and I wasn't letting myself down. **Friendly winks from John Terry my captain and the odd 'well done Timmy' from Frank Lampard made me proud in my blue shirt.**

Seconds left. A corner for Leeds. An inswinger. Petr Cech comes for it. He misses. Cresswell heads it goalward. He's already celebrating. I stretch out a leg and as the ball is about to cross the line deflect it to safety.

The final whistle goes. We're through.

I've had this dream with countless different Chelsea line-ups. In fact, by my reckoning I'm the only player that's played in every Chelsea team for the last 15 years. While I'm having these dreams, it's the greatest feeling in the world. But then I wake up and face the disappointment that I never made it as a professional footballer…

My football career started as an eight-year-old when I moved to Chorleywood and met Matt Thomson, the boy who would go on to become Matt Milan, the male model and stalwart of the Mighty Badgers. We quickly became good friends and one day he suggested I go with him to cubs, not because I expressed an interest in dib-dib-dibbing but because they had a football team. I wasn't interested in camping or tying knots; I just wanted to play football. Trouble was at the end of our weekly meeting, the leaders used to get a ball out and make us play crab football. If you're not familiar with the game, crab football is where you sit on the floor with your arms behind you and then try to play football like a crab. What a frustrating game. It was like having a beautiful naked woman standing in front of you and you're not allowed to go anywhere near her. Utterly pointless.

But it was worth all the woggles and bob-a-jobbing just to get a real game of football. I played for 5th Rickmansworth, or 5th Ricky as everyone called us. We played in AC Milan shirts (black and red stripes) but had black shorts and socks, which never seemed quite right. Our main rivals were Eagles who played in old Leeds United kits, all white with the badge on. Sadly, this was the same kit I wore when I played for the cub representative side which may explain why there's a picture of me wearing a Leeds shirt in this book.

When I turned up at cubs I also met Paul Clarke who was one of the greatest cub players of his generation. His dad ran a team and they had one place left in the team at right back and even though I, like every other player, wanted to play midfield or up front. My misgivings were overruled by the fact that I was so desperate to play. So I became a defender by default and it wasn't until I reached secondary school that I finally got a chance to play midfield.

We had a guy at 5th Ricky called Chris Good who used to play upfront and I'm not exaggerating, but he must have been double our height. That said he came from a great footballing family and he was a very tidy player himself, so good that he went on to play for Brentford. Chris's ability, combined with his height was the most amazing advantage back then. We used to win matches 10, 11, 12–0, and Chris would always score nine or ten goals. It was ridiculous. But every team seemed to have a Chris Good. Our rival cub pack, 11th Ricky, had Simon Fox and he was banging in eight or more goals a week. Looking back, it was a bit of joke really. When I moved up to secondary school, we started to take football more seriously, even though we had possibly the worst kit I've ever worn. It was a green shirt, black shorts and, wait for it, orange socks. Come on, who plays in orange socks? It was like eleven goalkeepers running round the pitch. We used to play our games on Saturday morning and me and Matt Milan were good enough to play for the first XI even though we were two years younger. We were so good that we even beat Tim Sherwood's team once in the Cup and he was the greatest schoolboy player in the Watford area.

I was quite impressionable back then. I got a call one day from a mate who told me that a few of them were going to play for Wymax in Maple Cross. 'Why?' I asked him. 'Barry Redfearn's dad's taken over the team and he's brought a brand new shiny kit. It's sky blue with a v-neck.' 'Count me in,' I said and we all left Chorleywood Boys.

It's only when you leave school that the amateur game takes on a different guise. Gone are the days of youthful exuberance and carefree football and in comes the angry, ugly and violent world of Sunday League soccer. I started playing for a team called The Gatecrashers, run by Tony Bennett, or 'TB' as we all called him. Credit where credit's due, he turned us into a great team. We had some quality players chip up on a Sunday morning. But the problem with playing on a Sunday is that it often descended into a brawl. So not only did you have to contend with rock hard pitches, freezing weather and a hangover, but there was nearly always some player on the opposition who threatened to kill you after the final whistle. It was horrendous . . . and was hardly surprising. Most people, me included, often turned up to play on the Sunday morning still drunk from the night before, reeking of booze and having had only two hours sleep. I lost count of the number of times I saw people throwing up in the toilets before we ran out. And let me tell you, that first time you headed the ball was a pain unlike anything else. But what happened when you finished the game? You went to the pub again. That's Sunday League football for you.

It was around this time that I went to Northwood Town FC and demanded a trial. I can't believe I did that now but they let me try out and I managed to get in their reserve team. Northwood was a class apart. When you played a game, your shirt would be hanging up in the dressing room for you when you got there and you got five quid petrol expenses too after away matches. It's the closest I've come to being paid to play football. But I don't think the manager really liked me there and my suspicions were confirmed when I arrived one day and he just came out and told me there was no place for me today. As I started to head back to the car park, he called me back and told me that the first team were a man down and were looking for a sub if I fancied it.

'Where are they playing?' I asked.

'Beckton,' he replied. So I got in my Renault 5 and drove all the way to Beckton in East London, arriving just in time. I raced in the dressing room, introduced myself, got changed and took my place on the bench. Five minutes into the game, though, and one of our players goes down injured. And what do you know, it's the right midfielder; my position. It was like a dream. For me, that is, not the injured player. So on I went and I did really well. Nothing fancy, just winning the ball and laying it off. The next week they asked me back. I felt like I had made it, not least because this was a semi-pro team where some of the players were getting decent money.

But it didn't last. Three games later the injured player came back and I ended up back in the reserves, followed soon after by another demotion to the reserves of the reserves. With me getting nowhere fast at Northwood, I decided to jump ship and join Amersham but even then it had dawned on me that I was never going to make it as a professional player. Football just didn't seem the same any more.

It was only when me and my mates decided to start an old boys team, the Old Danes, that I rediscovered the joy of playing once more. We played in a green and white Celtic shirt, white shorts and white socks. It was brilliant playing for the Old Danes because when we joined the league they put us in a division two below the top one, but as we had so many great players in our team we just strolled it. We even made a law in the dressing room before one of the matches that you could only score from a header or a volley, so we ended up with all our players in the opposition penalty area trying to tee themselves up just to get on the scoresheet. What a laugh.

Saturday afternoon football with the Old Danes was the best. You'd get up in the morning, play with your mates in the afternoon, listen to the football results on the way to the pub and then carry on drinking all the way through. Before getting up the following morning and playing again for another team despite feeling like death. Just thinking of the Danes gives me a warm glow. We didn't have a manager in the end and we just played the way we wanted to play. Everybody was a good player, everybody knew what they were doing and we all got along. Sadly, the Danes dissolved when a few of the boys left but it was such a special time that I could still get up every Saturday and do it now if I had the chance.

BALL WATCHING

There was a time in my life when I always had a football with me, and I mean always. Even when I finally got my own flat I filled it with footballs (a) because I could, and (b) because there's something magic just walking around the place knocking a ball about. Even now as I write, I can see four footballs in front of me. There's a world cup ball, an old antique ball, that silver Nike one signed by Rivaldo (or rather, was signed by Rivaldo, until my daughter washed it off) and a Nike Premiership one. They're not for decoration either. They are footballs, therefore they are for kicking.

A good football is a thing of great beauty. When we were kids one of us would always have a leather ball and we would play on the concrete or in car parks with it until the leather panels started to peel off and you'd be left playing with little more than a partially inflated bladder.

Those balls were great. They were only ever semi-inflated because nobody had a pump or could be bothered to bring one along and when they got wet they became so heavy that when you headed them your brains ached for hours afterwards. Whenever anybody got a new ball, they would always do their best to stop anybody kicking it on the concrete just to protect the leather. But resistance was futile. Within a week or two, the ball would have been used and abused in hundreds of games of World Cup or Volley In the Wally with Tim and Jonathan Kissel and Duncan Patterson in St Andrews Church car park and would have gone the same, scuffed way as every other leather ball we ever had.

Balls are amazing things, and I always have one in the boot of my car. I remember being in Northampton town centre once, and I had a ball on me. Me and a group of friends decided to try out an experiment and see what would happen if we threw a ball up the high street at pub kicking-out time. What happened was incredible – it was just like the Carlsberg advert on TV, and it turned into a mass football kickabout. When anyone sees a ball in the world they have to kick it, apart from one country. I was in LA one year on holiday with a couple of mates, Stuart Saunders and Andy Wallace. It was overcast, so we decided to go to Venice Beach and have a kickabout. What disturbed us was that whenever we kicked the ball into the path of the locals, they picked it up, rather than instinctively kicking it back. When they did try and kick it, it ended up in the sea. David Beckham has his work cut out.

The great thing about football is you can have an impromptu game anywhere. All you need is a beautiful ball and some people. I once nearly got put in an overnight cell for playing football in a petrol station. It wasn't the playing in the station that landed me in hot water, it was swearing at the policeman who was trying to stop us playing.

DEEP DOWN
I STILL THINK I'VE GOT IT

On *Soccer AM*, we were constantly banging on about how rubbish my co-presenter Helen Chamberlain's team Torquay were so one day the club called in and invited me to go along and train with them. I was dreading it but I agreed and turned up wearing my golden football boots because I knew it would wind everyone up. When I got out on the training pitch, though, I looked at the team and their faces said it all. I was destined for a kicking. Sure enough, they absolutely hammered me and there were two or three 50–50 balls that were very nasty. That said, apart from their fitness levels, I think I more than held my own. I even scored a couple of goals and celebrated with a few cartwheels. That went down well. Seriously, though, training with a professional side was one of the best experiences of my life. Torquay treated me well and the lads down there were brilliant. As a kid you're always led to believe that if you're going to make it as a professional you have to be truly gifted and stand out from the crowd but that night, as we drove home after a few beers (we got a lift home), me and Fenners agreed that there was absolutely no reason why we shouldn't have been professional footballers.

18

HARD FOUGHT LESSONS OF A FOOTBALL FAN

When you watch as much football as I do, you see at first hand the many, varied emotions that the football fan goes through. At Chelsea those emotions tend be ones of great joy and happiness, but elsewhere, like at Leeds, it's probably despair and dejection.

But when you think about it, there are only three real types of fan that watch the game. First, there is the optimist, which is what I like to think I am. My attitude is based on complete belief in the Chelsea players and management, which given that we've got a great, successful squad, packed with world class international players is, not surprisingly, a bit easier than it would be supporting Bury. I never worry about our opponents. Never.

Then there is the pessimist. This is the type of person who may be a Manchester United fan, the reigning champions, but still frets when they've got a home FA Cup tie against Torquay. They could be walking the league by 20 points, in the Champions' League and have a full strength, in form side out and they would still be sat there, going 'I've got a funny feeling about this one, you know.' Sadly, most England fans now fit into this category. Even if we are nothing like it with our club sides, we suddenly all change when it comes to England. I have tried my utmost in my columns and on television shows to get people thinking positively about England but it's just so hard. Every one has a bad feeling about England all the time these days. It's sad. For the record, all football journalists fall into this category.

Finally, there is the angry fan. This is the man who rather than celebrate a goal prefers to turn to the opposition fans and give them the bird. We've all seen him. When the ball goes in he'll grab his mate by the neck with one hand, clench his other fist with the other and then abuse the away fans. It's not 'Brilliant! We've scored!' It's 'Take that you dirty w****s*&!$!!!!' In fact, I suspect they're only truly happy when they're angry. My brother was like that. In everyday life he was perfectly normal but as soon as the ref blew to start the game he would mutate into Mr Angry and this completely irrational rage would take over him. It was like a Jekyll and Hyde response to the referee's whistle. One peep and he was off.

Whatever type of fan you are, once you've signed up to support a club, you'll immediately receive your club blinkers. That means you start believing that ALL decisions go against your team, every referee is biased against your club and you will have ludicrous arguments as to why your club is better than somebody else's. A great example of this is Tom Watt, better known to some of you as Lofty from Eastenders. He has to be one of Arsenal's biggest fans. To give Tom his due, he knows everything there is to know about football and has an encyclopedic knowledge of Arsenal. I was with him at an event a couple of years ago when Chelsea were well on their way to winning the league for the first time since 1955 and didn't look like they could lose it. When I told Tom how happy I was with Chelsea's success he piped up with: 'You might win the league but we've got Flamini, Fabregas and Van Persie coming through so I'd rather be in my shoes than in yours.' He genuinely believed this. That, in a nutshell, is your club blinkers.

DON'T **HATE**
GLORY **HUNTERS**

If you're jealous of Man Utd, Chelsea and Arsenal's success over recent years, I urge you to think again because, although as a Chelsea fan I've become accustomed to success over recent years, I actually think that staying up is a much better feeling than winning the league. I've been there when the Blues avoided the drop by beating Leeds at Stamford Bridge. I remember Ken Bates saying: 'if this is how we feel when we stay up, what will it feel like when we win the league?'

When success finally came our way and we won the FA Cup I remember going to Stamford Bridge to see the trophy being paraded through the streets and found myself resenting all the little kids with their hats and scarves on. These nippers had only been following Chelsea, following football even, for a few years and they had already tasted success. They hadn't suffered like me. Don't get me wrong, it was great to see this sea of colour around the ground and all these happy young faces but I couldn't help thinking 'you lucky gits'.

But I do think there is something much more pleasurable about supporting a team that doesn't do well. If you're a fan of a team that never wins anything, never goes anywhere, it really feels like you're doing your bit and feels like you're a much more intrinsic part of the club. It's this wonderful, humble feeling you have, like you're doing your bit for charity. Helen Chamberlain knows this feeling very well.

Even though I wouldn't change what I've seen at Chelsea over the years, there is something magical about supporting your boys when they are going through hell. I'm really looking forward to this season because Chelsea are no longer the favourites and the pressure is all on Man Utd. I've spoken to some of my United and Arsenal friends and they agree that fighting for the title is more satisfying than winning it and keeping it. What it is about not being successful I don't know, but sometimes I think it would be quite nice to be a City fan. Then I came to my senses and thank God I'm not.

UNDERSTAND THAT HOME ADVANTAGE IS CLAPTRAP

When I used to travel with Chelsea it was always more fun than going to the home game but it doesn't always seem that way for the team. In fact, I have never quite understood the idea of home advantage. Surely whatever pitch you play on will be the same size and standard for both sides? There may be different little tricks they pull in the changing rooms where they may make the away one a little bit pokier and paint it in dull, uninspirational colours but at the big clubs like Manchester United and Arsenal, the dressing rooms are equal size – they have to be so they can host international matches and semi-finals. At the top level, then, the only difference is that the away team is faced with a load of squawking home fans shouting the odds.

The only way home advantage could ever technically be construed as an advantage was when teams like Luton, Oldham, Queens Park Rangers and Preston decided to play on plastic pitches at their grounds rather than grass. Then, when the opposition teams arrived, they found themselves chasing a ball that bounced and bounced and never came down while the home side knew exactly what was going to happen. It was hysterical.

If you look back at how successful the teams with plastic pitches were it was ridiculous and all because they'd played on the kind of shoddy artificial grass they used on garage forecourts or for butcher's displays and nobody else did. As fans, we all used to say that it was clearly an advantage having an artificial pitch but the authorities just couldn't see it. I remember John Gregory telling me that when he was at QPR as a player, they used to watch the opposition trying out the pitch for the first time and there would always be one player who threw himself into a sliding tackle, only to get up with third degree carpet burns on his legs.

Of course, home advantage can turn into a disadvantage too. Look at Nottingham Forest. When Brian Clough was boss he took a team from the old Second Division, first to promotion, then to the First Division title and then to two famous European Cup wins. I was told by one ex-Forest player, who shall remain nameless, that he hated running out at the City Ground with all the fans looking at them and going 'Our team won the European Cup twice, you lot aren't fit to wear the shirt…' But you can understand how those fans felt because it wasn't so long ago that they were in the Premiership. The same player, by the way, also told me that when he was at Forest he would prefer the away games because the team were more appreciated by the crowd.

There are other exceptions to the rule, though, especially when a team like Chelsea is playing a lower league side in a cup competition. Last season, for example, as soon as the Blues got drawn against Norwich in the fifth round of FA Cup at Stamford Bridge you may as well have drawn our quarter-final opponents there and then as well. There was no way we were ever going to lose that match and we didn't. We won 4–0.

The point is that lower league teams, for want of a better phrase, can often get a result in these kind of matches on their own turf, where the pitch is different and the crowd are right on top of the players, but the likelihood of any minnow now travelling to a team like Liverpool or Manchester United and causing an upset is virtually nil these days.

Some people say the Football Association should mix it up a bit. That it would it be a good idea for all Premiership teams in the FA Cup having to play away whenever they're drawn against a lower league side, regardless of what team comes out of the velvet bag first. Maybe then you'd see a few more upsets . . . But I think the beauty of the Cup is there are no seeded teams, it's completely fair, apart from the fact that some of the balls are hot and some of them in the bag are cold. Only joking!

LOYAL SUPPORTERS

I got into a cab the other day and the driver recognised me from the telly so thought he'd tell me about the state of modern English football. At length . . .

He was a Spurs fan and he claimed that the day when Sol Campbell left to join their bitter rivals Arsenal was the day he realised that there was no loyalty left in the sport.

The cabbie also thought that Steve Bruce, no stranger to having his loyalty questioned after jumping managerial ships several times before joining Birmingham, was also being disloyal by deserting the Brummies for Wigan.

And he didn't stop there either!

He banged on and on about Ashley Cole leaving Arsenal for Chelsea, William Gallas going the other way, coach Frank Arnesen leaving Spurs to go to Chelsea and Liam Ridgwell going to Birmingham from Villa. All these examples showed how there was no loyalty in football and it was all utterly disgraceful.

I thought about what he was saying and realised that as football fans, we all love to think that our players are not actually there working doing a job and supporting themselves, but are playing for the love of putting our team's shirt on and wearing the club badge over their hearts.

I never know what to think of this because obviously as fans we'd all gladly play for our clubs for free – I'd definitely still do a job for Chelsea just in front of the back four and they wouldn't have to pay me for the privilege!

But when it's your job, and your income, and you potentially only have 10 years at the top, then money must enter the equation and as fans we should acknowledge this.

Once, Craig Hignett took a paycut to stay at 'Boro so he could play top-flight football and it paid off for him as he ended up having a great career.

I think we've got to have an open mind and realise that even though it's not the way we'd like it as supporters, footballers are only doing a job, albeit the finest one in the world.

The cabbie was still going on about how the game had gone to pot and why should we care about our teams, if the players don't care about the club and are only in it for the money. When he'd finally piped down I asked him how often he went to White Hart Lane.

'Oh, I've not been there for years!' he said. 'On the weekends, I have to look after the kids and I've got other stuff to do so I watch them on telly every now and then.'

THE 1980s

Thank God that in modern times going to football is generally a pleasant experience. Writing this book has brought back a lot of memories of watching the game in the 1980s and how it was a genuinely scary event. Whenever you took your place on the terraces there was always this menacing undercurrent, this sense that something unpleasant was going to happen. You'd often be on the terraces terrified that you'd be stood next to a group of the oppo's fans that were about to burst into a song and, before you knew it, you'd be in the thick of a full-on ruck.

But I never really got violence. Maybe that's because I'm a rubbish fighter and, if the truth be known, I'm a bit of a chicken. Sure, I understood the feeling of being part of a travelling army, for want of a better word, but going from that to beating up complete strangers in another part of the country just never made sense. Besides, all I ever saw was groups of blokes egging each other on, then advancing a few paces, throwing a few punches before retreating really quickly and then doing it again.

Remember, this was the age when you could still pay at the turnstile and get in (like I did at the 1983 FA Cup Final Replay between Brighton and Man Utd); when police used to escort you to and from the ground; when away fans used to be kept in after the final whistle for their own safety, and when running on the pitch still wasn't a criminal offence. Actually, on that last point I should confess that I also used to run on to the pitch after Chelsea goals and while other blokes ran on trying to incite the opposition fans, I used to do cartwheels and forward rolls. That's right, other fans went on looking for trouble. I practised my gymnastics, much to the amusement of Ginger. But people forget that fans used to go on the pitch after every goal and celebrate with the players. This is why it became fashionable to sit in the stands where there were no fences, rather than stand in the terraces, long before all-seated stadiums.

Yes, all the grounds that you would expect to be hugely intimidating often were but to be honest, I have felt threatened at places all over the country. Looking back, I don't know why we bothered putting ourselves through the agony of trying to survive a football match. Me and Ginger once went up to Villa Park for a Chelsea game and the atmosphere was hostile to say the least. Come the end of the game, we stayed put, expecting to be kept in for a while, which was tradition for away fans so they can clear the streets and prevent fighting. Only on this day, the ref blew and the coppers and stewards started ushering us out into the mean streets of Birmingham and they were just like 'You're free to go.'

'But I don't want to go!' I was thinking. 'I want to be kept in for an hour . . .'

Too late. We were already outside and then it's half hour of trying to look your hardest to avoid getting caught up in any sort of trouble.

Some away grounds were just so intimidating, so vicious, that I ended up inventing excuses just to avoid going. I had a long list of them . . .

'Hey Tim, Spurs on Saturday. You coming up?'

'Can't, I'm gutted.'

'Why not?'

'Er, it's my nan's birthday . . .'

'But it was your nan's birthday six weeks ago when we played West Ham away . . .'

'Hey Tim, we've got Millwall away in the Cup. You coming?'

'Yeah, love to, but it's a total nightmare, my cousin's coming down to visit.'

'But you haven't got a cousin . . .'

Fortunately, I have only ever been the victim of a random act of violence just once and it wasn't even at a Chelsea match. Another mate of mine suggested we go and watch a Watford game at Norwich and with nothing better to do I agreed. Anyway, we went to the match and everything was fine but when we left the ground I was walking along the street when this bloke just walked up to me and smacked me in the mouth for no reason. I hadn't said a word. I never gave him a nasty look. Nothing. He just belted me. Clearly, I hadn't realised the decades of hostility that existed between the Hornets and the Canaries stretching back to the infamous incident . . . Er, hang on, there isn't one. Sadly, I reckon I was just in the wrong place at the wrong time.

Because of fan violence it was no wonder attendances plummeted. And the decline in violence has coincided with the explosion in football attendances over the last decade in this country. But the reason being inside a football stadium is safe today is because of the invention of CCTV camera which gives the police the opportunity to pinpoint and arrest troublemakers. Of course, you'll still get a few loudmouths now and then shouting the odds but, mercifully, it's a million miles away from what it used to be like.

DON'T BE AFRAID
TO FOLLOW OTHER CLUBS

When you've supported a club for as long as I have there are certain players that you end up following wherever they go. Not literally, of course – that would be stalking – but in terms of the new clubs that they move on to. But that in itself presents its own problems.

Take Dennis Wise. When he was at Chelsea he was always one of my favourite players. Determined, skilful and more than a little volatile, Wisey always gave it everything he had, sometimes to his own detriment, and quickly endeared himself to the Stamford Bridge faithful. When he finally left in 2001 (after 11 years at the club) he moved on to Leicester City. That was fine but it was the move after that that made things difficult because seventeen games and one pre-season bust-up later Wisey moved on . . . to Millwall.

Now with Wisey at the helm at the New Den, Milllwall had become the team I had a strange fondness for, for the first time in my life. What was going on? They're London rivals. Somehow, though, when you like a player, when you really like a player, and you want them to do well you can see past everything and still support them. So what happens is that once you know the Chelsea result, you start looking for the Millwall score just to see how Wisey got on.

Today, of course, not only is Wisey at Leeds but he's taken Gus Poyet, another of my all-time Chelsea favourites, with him. It's like he's doing it on purpose. How can I support them now when they're at a club that I have a lifelong rivalry with? Because Wisey and Gus are true professionals, proper football people and top men to boot. And now I really hope they get out of League One.

But I'm just like every other football fan; I have the players and teams I like and those that I don't. The sad thing about being a Chelsea fan is that we don't really have a derby game to enjoy each season. Perhaps the closest we have, or rather had, was whenever we played Leeds United. Leeds, you see, are the same as us. There's any number of teams in Yorkshire that they play that could be considered a derby but none of those matches compare to, say, a Chelsea or a Man Utd match. That's why after the hotly contested FA Cup Finals of 1970 the two teams seemed to latch on to each other.

When Leeds went down to the Championship I was really sad because I always enjoyed the rivalry between the two teams, as did the players. Lucas Radebe even brought me a Leeds shirt signed by all the team when he came on *Soccer AM*. It was always a unique atmosphere at the Bridge when Leeds visited. To see them go down again though was even worse and now they've had 15 points deducted too; that's hard to take, especially for the fans.

It's always sad when a club of such stature plummets through the leagues but I have a feeling that Leeds will be like Manchester City and not only get back to the Premier League but get back and prosper. It may not seem like that for Leeds supporters at the moment but they've got too much history and too many fans to just fade away. They'll be back and sooner rather than later.

THE COLOUR OF YOUR KIT IS KEY

While many people cynically view football kits as mere marketing or money-making tools, I believe their significance goes far, far beyond that. You see, your football shirt is a badge of honour and a symbol of allegiance. It is an open and public statement that this is who you are this is the team I support. Especially if it's that chocolate-coloured one that Coventry had in the 70s which is one of the best kits ever.

Over the years, I have carried out a lot of research into the colours of football kits and it's a fascinating subject. No, really. Anyway, I'm now prepared to reveal my findings and I have concluded that it is those teams that play in red that stand the greatest chance of success.

The reason for this is that red makes things look closer to you, whereas blue makes things seem further away. That's why the most successful teams in English football history are Liverpool, Manchester United and Arsenal. Even Nottingham Forest, who won two European Cups, wore red. Of course, what that does suggest is that in winning the league in a blue kit Chelsea have actually achieved more than any of their red-shirted rivals. In short, it means more when Chelsea wins the title. Ha ha.

Clearly, the colour of a team's kit is of paramount importance to their performance. Everyone remembers when Alex Ferguson blamed Man Utd's 3–1 defeat at Southampton on the grey kits they were wearing but, as usual, he was right because it was really difficult to pick out the United players as the game was continuing. When Arsenal went the whole season undefeated, they started the following campaign with a new kit that was more of a plum colour than the typical pillar-box red you associate with them. What happened? They struggled badly. I remember telling my Arsenal mates that it was the wrong kit and they laughed it off, but I was right. And to rub it in, Chelsea won the title.

Recently, Chelsea has addressed the visibility problem of their blue kits by introducing a luminous kit. It was a good move. I have always thought a luminous kit was a sensible idea ever since I went to Stamford Bridge to watch Chelsea v Barcelona and Barca came out in their Day-Glo yellow one. I remember sitting there looking at the pitch and thinking that not only could I not pick out the Chelsea players in their blue kit but all I could really see was a mass of yellow all over the pitch. Even when I ride my scooter around town the only motorbikes you can see out of the corner of your eye is the ones with the riders wearing the luminous vests.

Mark my words, the fluorescent kit is the future. Soon, every club will have a shirt so dazzling you'll have to wear shades when the teams run out. It'll be like watching twenty-two giant highlighter pens running around for ninety minutes. Either that or they'll be outlawed in the same way that steroids are for giving you an unfair advantage.

White kits are an altogether different proposition. Yes, I know Real Madrid have won many things in their history and Leeds did alright in the late 60s and early 70s and Aston Villa won the European Cup in their white away shirts but white, let me tell you, is a passive, uninspiring colour and these teams tend to succeed despite their shirts and not because of them.

Quite where claret and blue comes into my theory, though, is anybody's guess…

6-0-6

Having done 6-0-6 all this season I've had more of an understanding of what being a football fan is all about. As you know I'm an optimist and always believe that my team are going to win. However, the duty of a football fan is to moan and the job of the football phone-in show is to air these grievances. The expression that football fans have to use the most is 'But...'. For example, 'We're ten points ahead at the top of the league, we're playing the best football I've ever seen, but I'm worried about the left hand side on the field, or the owners, or whether we've got strength in depth in the squad, or the temperament of our striker.' The football fan never sees perfection, and I think is never happier than when things are going against their team.

I apologize to West Brom fans, I have half a dozen friends who support the Baggies and they epitomize the fans who moan the most. Even during their run-in to promotion, they were miserable, and one of them, a lovely girl called Jadeen, actually admitted at one stage that she'd rather not go up and justified it with some ludicrous explanation about losing matches in the Premiership.

Now, I understand what she means. I'm going to say something that you all think is barmy. I'm quite envious of Leeds United fans.

As a football fan, there's something really lovely about adversity. As Man City fans showed a few seasons ago, when they were playing in the lower tiers of English football, more than 30,000 fans turned up every week and probably had the time of their lives as City made the play-offs and won an incredibly dramatic final at Wembley.

Leeds are now in a position where the only way is up, and sticking together in these troubled times gives you a wonderful feeling.

Possibly, one of the greatest times of supporting Chelsea was beating Leeds many moons ago to stay in the top flight – what a great feeling that was. We'd had a rubbish season but then beat our old rivals to stay up on an amazing night.

I'm not saying that supporters of smaller clubs have it better as they probably never have a chance of glory, but for teams who once tasted the big time - like Leeds United who reached the Champions League semi-final just six years ago – to plumb the depths then bounce back will be an amazing journey.

When Chelsea won the Premiership for the first time it was an amazing season but the defence of the title was nowhere near as much fun. Man Utd fans don't know what it's like to have the wonderful feeling of adversity followed by triumph.

19

MONEY: THE ROOT OF ALL BRILLIANCE

This is the chapter that will get right up the fundamentalist, or 'real fan's' nose. For some reason, they have no understanding of basic economics and any mention of money is like a red rag to a bull. I think the sad thing about the modern day football fan is that they are obsessed with money. I would go as far as to say they are even more obsessed than the footballers themselves. For instance, you get fans of lower division clubs now saying that they're glad of the away tie they've been given at Old Trafford rather than a home draw because it will help balance the books. Good business maybe, but that's the end of their cup run. Or you'll have fans saying absurd things like 'we may have sold our best player but it was good business'. Who cares about business? Or how about 'we don't want to go down because we'll lose our share of the Sky money'. So what, you'll be playing in a lower division. I think as a football fan it is your duty to leave your finances to your chairman and to concentrate on enjoying the football.

Money in football is a hot topic. A couple of years ago, I wrote a piece for a London newspaper in which I argued that the legion of millionaire footballers at work in the Premiership were, in fact, grossly UNDERPAID. To say it was an unpopular stance was an understatement. Later, the paper told me that they'd never had as many letters and emails about an article they had run. I won't be so crude as to say exactly what most of the letters called me but suffice to say I certainly hit a nerve.

But I stand by every word of it. Why? Because compared to stars in the world of entertainment they get paid a pittance. Look at how much Tom Cruise gets paid. Whenever he churns out another movie he banks a gazillion dollars and yet any of us can act. We've all done school plays, haven't we? How difficult was that? Or what about Bono? He's absolutely loaded and all because he wears a cowboy hat and some sunglasses and sings a few songs. I doubt if he works more than a month or two a year.

But footballers, you have to understand, are both supremely talented athletes AND entertainers. They give us entertainment and enjoyment, week in, week out for forty weeks of the year. They also generate a hell of a lot of money. So if you have a player who can score you thirty goals a season and take you to the Champions' League final, or one that keeps you in the Premiership with all the financial benefits that entails, how can you possibly say he's not worth the money he's getting? Let's face it, elite footballers don't get paid as much as Formula One drivers. They don't get paid as much as the world's best golfers, tennis players or boxers either. And yet football is the premier sport in the world.

Besides, they are entitled to earn as much as they can from their careers, aren't they? Why should footballers be treated differently from any other occupation? If you were offered the chance to leave your job and then double your salary at a rival company you would be gone in a flash. But if a footballer does it, they're accused of being a 'Judas'. It's like you are not allowed to accept a pay rise or better your standard of living. You will stay at this club until you can no longer play.

Even the way people talk about footballer's wages is different to everybody else. When anybody else takes a job their salary is talked about in annual terms but footballers? No, their wages are weekly. Only cleaners and barmen and people in lower-end jobs talk about their wages in weekly terms. You don't hear City fat cats saying their earn £250,000 a week, do you? So why do they do it? Because the newspapers know that if you talk about their money in £100,000 a week it just seems more ostentatious than saying £5 million a year. Which, incidentally, is less than a movie star gets for a couple of weeks work on a film. What you have got to remember is that these people have wives and kids and like anyone else in any other walk of life all they are trying to do is further themselves. Yes, a lot of footballers are earning a lot of money but it's only the ones at the top of the game. Remember the ones lower down in the league that are driving round in Fiat Unos desperately trying to make ends meet. The only big money is at the top.

So when Will Smith gives me as much entertainment as John Terry or Stevie Gerrard or when Mick Jagger latches onto a loose ball and lashes in a half-volley from outside the box then, and only then, will we talk. Until such time, I'm standing my ground.

YOUNG AT HEART

I feel for young footballers these days. Yes, they get exceptionally well paid and they're doing a job that most of us, me included, would love to do, but they're also under a lot of pressure to be 'role models' for the nation's young people. Correct me if I'm wrong but isn't that the jobs of mums and dads and not Wayne Rooney or Theo Walcott?

Just because a player is young, rich and in the public eye, why does it suddenly become their job to lead the life of the righteous? We have this ridiculous idea in this country that because footballers are paid a lot of money they are not allowed to have a good time, not allowed to get drunk, not allowed to pull women and not allowed to drive fast cars because WE OWN THEM. They are our players and as such they are not allowed to do anything that is remotely interesting or, for that matter, vaguely normal. Do young rock 'n' roll stars have to deal with the same pressure, especially when their behaviour is invariably worse? Yes, footballers need to set a good example – that's a given – but the young players also need the space to enjoy their youth, just like every other kid in the country.

That ridiculous term 'role model' is always over-used. Why should a 19-year-old boy be a role model to your children? It's just not fair. As I've always said, I got my morals off my mum and dad, not Kerry Dixon. If you're blaming footballers for your children's behaviour, I suggest you go back to parent school.

DON'T BLAME THE PLAYERS

These days, you cannot pick up a newspaper without reading about a professional footballer doing something wrong.

It used to just be the tabloids with sensational stories about young Premier League stars' wrongdoings, but it's now open season on footballers in every national newspaper.

As you know, I'm a fan of modern football and never like listening to too much criticism of our beautiful game. But, right now, the game I love is actually getting a terrible hammering in the tabloid press for the lack of discipline among its players.

Often, you'll read how the young players have a responsibility to be role models but I think that's unfair. Footballers should be able to enjoy themselves and make mistakes as much as me or any of you reading this book.

However, I feel the real problem may lie with the absence of senior professionals at so many clubs these days. Back in the day, the manager ran the team and the senior pro would give the youngsters a bit of a battering, literally and physically, if they ever dared to overstep the mark.

A great example of this in modern football, was Roy Keane who apparently ruled Man United with an iron fist. If you were a young player at Old Trafford who'd played a handful of first-team games and turned up to the ground driving a Bentley or wearing a diamond encrusted Rolex or were giving it large around Manchester, you'd be more than just cleaning his boots as a result.

As I understand it, ex-United players like Brian McClair used to get the juniors to pick them up and take them to and from training every day or even shopping if they wanted to. Even though this sounds archaic I suppose it instilled some sort of responsibility in the young players.

Keane's now in management, and other former senior pros like Tony Adams, Paul Ince and Stuart Pearce are involved in coaching or management as well. None of whom would ever have stood for any nonsense from the younger players.

Nowadays, with so much talent on display, the senior pro is generally a thing of the past and the young pups are able to do what they want without it being questioned.

I have to say that I don't think this is their fault.

The clubs and management need to take responsibility for educating, disciplining and controlling the players. And that doesn't mean sell them if you think they'll cause trouble as that doesn't solve anything.

SHIRT CHANG£D

Hands up who thinks football shirts are a rip-off? Well I don't and here's why. Say a football shirt is £45 and you give that shirt to your son for his birthday. Now, if they were anything like me when I was a kid they will wear that shirt every minute of every hour of every day if they're allowed to and God help you if you try to take it off them to wash it. Now say a football shirt is £45 and you, as an adult, have bought it for yourself. You will wear it to every home game and to several away games. You will wear it to the pub during the week. You will wear it around the house. You may even wear it to bed. In my eyes, that represents brilliant value.

If you go and buy yourself a shirt from a designer shop, the chances are that it will be out of fashion in six months and it will probably cost you a lot more than a football shirt. Football shirts, on the other hand, never go out of fashion because they're actually above fashion and what's more, clubs will only change them once every two years. Also, if you do wear a shirt from a few seasons ago it proves that you're not some Johnny Come Lately, giving you extra credence as a fan. On top of everything, the football shirt is extremely comfortable. In fact, round my house, it's always been a running joke with my ex-wife, because I wear football shirts and shorts around the house. I just feel at home in them.

Of course parents get harassed by their kids to buy the new club shirt but then they get harassed by their kids for everything from sweets to trainers to iPods. If parents do find themselves struggling to find the money to buy the new kit they should do what my mum used to do and say, 'No'. Instead it's all 'Oh no, Boro have got three shirts this year! How much is that going to cost me?' Well, nothing if you don't buy it!

As with most things, Manchester United seem to bear the brunt of the criticism over replica shirts but what are they really guilty of? Satisfying a demand for a product by supplying it? Take them down. It's as if basic economics should not apply when it comes to football. If a band decide to sell four different style t-shirts on their world tour no-one will moan about that. It's up to you to buy as many as you want. If Topman can bring out as many t-shirts as they want, then why can't football teams? If they don't sell them, then that's their problem isn't it?

WINTER BREAKS ARE RUBBISH

During the winter, someone (usually Sven-Goran Eriksson) starts banging on about English football taking a break for the winter. You know, the usual stuff about allowing the players to be with their families over Christmas and giving them a well-earned rest and all that.

Nice in theory, but in practice, I reckon it would be a complete disaster.

One reason why winter breaks are crap, is because you get the best football over the festive season.

Like so many people, I was ill over Christmas with man flu and I couldn't get out of bed for 10 days, but I managed to watch loads of football matches.

On *Soccer Am*, I worked throughout the season without a break so I used to think it'd be good to have a rest, but now, as a fan again, I realise how good Christmas is for football as you can see matches all the time.

And it's a time where the big clubs can come unstuck as so many games are played in such a short space of time.

But, apart from the beauty of our Christmas fixtures, the other main reason winter breaks are rubbish I witnessed first hand on holiday in Dubai shortly after New Year. After spending Christmas in bed, I went to Dubai for a few days rest and relaxation – by the way, I didn't enjoy myself there as an hour after I arrived I saw Jade Goody by my pool and thought 'I don't belong here'.

Anyway, there was a match on in Dubai Stadium between Inter Milan and Ajax (who both play in leagues that have winter breaks), that was part of a tournament there so I thought I'd go down and watch it. The organisation was appalling as they were selling tickets out of an ice-cream van. When I finally managed to get in with a couple of hundred English people also on holiday, I witnessed a ridiculous, worse-than-pre-season-friendly exhibition match where both teams played half-heartedly.

I imagine these matches are supposed to be warm-ups to get players ready for the second halves of their seasons, but clearly they're moneymaking tours to promote the clubs around the world.

It has to be said, the Dubai locals absolutely loved the match and it's always great to see football abroad as a world sport.

But, if we did have a winter break, I doubt it would mean the players would spend time with their families and going out with their friends, as they'd be doing tours in the Far East, America and Dubai – and all we'd get for Christmas would be sub-standard exhibition matches rather than hard-fought Premier League games. I know what I'd rather have!

TAP TAP TAP...

Why does football have different laws to every other business in the world? More specifically, can anybody tell me what is wrong with so-called 'tapping up'? Imagine if you were approached by a rival company, offered a bit more money and a promotion? You'd be off, right? Well, why can't footballers do the same? It's just another example of football being a law unto itself. What are players expected to do? Sit around at a club they don't really want to be at, waiting for their contracts to expire? Not talk to someone who wants to employ them? It's ludicrous. If they got rid of the 'tapping up' law then the transfer market, bizarrely, would be much more transparent. Besides, if you looked after your players in the first place, they wouldn't want to leave.

BY LOYAL APPOINTMENT

Last year, the Reading club captain Graeme Murty signed a two-year extension to his deal at the club. His new contract meant that Murty would have spent ten years at the club, thereby entitling him to a testimonial. Or so he thought. When the deal was signed, the Reading chairman John Madejski publicly announced that Murty wouldn't be getting a testimonial. 'In days gone by,' he said, 'there was a reason for them because players were paid diddly squat. That is not the case now – they are paid an incredible amount of money.'

As far as I'm concerned, testimonials are awarded for loyalty and in this day and age where players move from club to club to club, having a player who stays at one club for ten years, and who doesn't benefit from his slice of all those transfer fees, is more or less unheard of. That surely deserves recognition. Remember, there is still a very small minority of players in this country who can actually retire from their earnings. They're not all minted. They don't all drive Baby Bentleys or Hummers.

OK, so a player in the Premiership may not actually need the money raised from a testimonial game but those who play in the lower leagues certainly do. Besides, supporters will be more likely to turn up for a game for a loyal servant of the club than they will for virtually any other reason.

But if you're lucky enough to be a millionaire Premiership player and you do have a testimonial, the best way to do it would be to spend a little money on getting the best players you can to turn up for the game, then take a little slice for yourself before giving a big chunk to charity, like Alan Shearer or Niall Quinn did. The only problem is with the players that have a testimonial and keep the lot. It's those players that need to have a good look at themselves.

TV, QUICK!

Here's a prediction. In a few years time, you will be able to watch any Premiership game you like on your TV or PC for a couple of quid. The way I see it, fans want to watch their teams, not spend time and money on a subscription to watch every other team but their own. You can almost do it now. Sky already show eight

Champions League games simultaneously and you can even get virtually all the Premiership games via the internet, via foreign satellites. With the line between TV and the internet becoming increasingly blurred and with so many more outlets available for fans to watch their football – you can even watch it on your mobile – I can't see any broadcaster paying the kind of money for TV rights that we've seen in recent years. Last time around Sky paid a bewildering £1.3 billion for the rights to live Premiership football. Trust me, it won't go any higher.

At this point I'd like to say, for those of you who hate all the money pouring into the modern game and think it's ruining football, try going to county cricket, speedway, or the dogs – all once-great sports but now in the doldrums because they have no money and tiny attendances. Depressing is not the word at these events. In any other business in the world, money coming in is seen as a good thing. Why should it be any different in football?

GIVE YOUR CHAIRMAN A BREAK

As a football fan, there is a law that states that you have to have a love-hate relationship with your chairman. When your chairman takes control and buys your club for a pound, taking all of the debt on, you have to be extremely wary. It doesn't matter if they are billionaires willing to give your team huge, great chunks of their personal fortune, it is still the football fan's job to be sceptical. It could be the Russian at Chelsea; the Thai bloke at Man City, the Americans at Liverpool or the Icelandic chap at West Ham; it doesn't matter. Chairmen, especially foreign ones, are always viewed with suspicion. They have always got some ulterior motive.

They are never in it for the long haul. The fundamentalists revel in this image, as though each new owner has come from the Death Star.

But this is rubbish. Look at the Glazers. When their takeover at Manchester United was going through you would have thought that they were nothing but a bunch of Americans intent on buying the club and then selling off Old Trafford to Tesco judging by the howl of protests from the fans. Within two seasons though, they had won the title again for the first time in four seasons and built a squad the envy of Europe.

Not many chairmen are liked. The ones who seem to get the most respect are the ones who support their clubs and stay out of the limelight. Men like Jack Walker at Blackburn. In fact, as far as I'm aware Jack Walker was the only chairman in the history of the game who's ever been liked. Here is a man who took his club from being hardly the most glamorous side in the world, shoved a load of his own money in, and then transformed them into the Premier League champions, restoring them to the former glories of the early 20th century.

Typically, though, the first thing you do when your club is in trouble is blame the chairman and if you are a chairman you have to be resilient beyond belief. Look at Deadly Doug Ellis. He stayed at Aston Villa for donkey's years despite being hated by the fans. I've lost count of the number of managers he must have seen off.

Personally speaking, I have a lot of respect for chairmen. After referees they have to be the most hated people in the game and I can never understand why. Remember, all that chairmen really are are wealthy fans who want to get involved. Only time will tell if all the takeovers have killed our game. However, I think football's too big to ever die.

THE 39TH GAME

This is going to shock a lot of you, but I'm not completely anti the 39th game. If football is going to continue to be the biggest sport in the world and the Premiership the best league, we have to keep evolving. It's very hard to embrace change, and I was one of the fans who was very anti-Champions League, as I thought it would be the death of our top-flight football. Clearly I was wrong with that, as we now all realize how brilliant it is. I was also anti the amount of live football matches on television, also under the misguided opinion that this would ruin football. However, it seems the more football there is, the bigger the sport gets. Clearly the 39th game, in its current state, is unworkable, and no other football federation I imagine will want a Premiership circus to roll into town, but I think we should be open-minded about these things. Remember, Liverpool are such a massive club because of their journeys through Europe in the 1980s establishing them as a world force, and Manchester United are also enormous because of their exposure around the world. To expose our whole league to other continents can only be a good thing.

The arguments against it, I always feel, are slightly trivial. The first one is that it would be unfair. Sadly, football is unfair as we can't predict weather conditions, pitch conditions, injury conditions, poor officiating, and cheating. And that's why we love our sport. The other big argument against taking football matches abroad is the overused 'what about the travelling fan?' cliché. It's occurred to me that the travelling fan is the most over-represented minority the world has ever seen. Such a small percentage of fans travel to away matches, and to deny them one seems irrelevant, and anyway, look at the Barmy Army. They embrace a trip abroad, maybe it would be good for the die hard to get his passport out and see a bit of the world. The other thing about the travelling fan is, needless to say, they pay their money, they are loyal and the game couldn't live without them, but please remember Hong Kong paid £100 million for the rights of the Premier League. I imagine this is the sort of income that has paid for Ronaldo, Ballack, Torres et cetera.

THIS IS WAR...

I've always been intrigued by the battle for supremacy between the football kit manufacturers. When I was a kid, all you tended to have was Admiral or Umbro making all the club and home nations' shirts. Today, it's Adidas and Nike slugging it out. And it's getting messy.

Matters have intensified in recent years. Look across the top nations in world football. Brazil, Holland and Portugal are Nike, while Argentina, Germany and France and Spain are Adidas. The two notable exceptions, of course, are Italy who ditched Kappa in favour of Puma before the last World Cup and rewarded their new supplier with an unexpected victory. And then there's England, who have stuck with Umbro for years now, although I suspect, being that it's the biggest-selling shirt in the world, that when the contract next comes up for renewal, Umbro may find it too difficult to hold off the advances of the big two. We'll see.

Even in club football it's a no-holds barred grudge match. Real Madrid are Adidas. Barcelona at Nike. Liverpool and Chelsea and Adidas. Man United and Arsenal are Nike. There is this relentless, never-ending battle for supremacy between the big brands that's gone from shirts to equipment to footwear. And it's only going to get worse.

With competition so intense, it's hardly surprising that Nike and Adidas scrap it out to sign the latest prodigy. Now, whenever a young player shows some signs of promise, they are snapped up immediately. Often, it will be a punt, a gamble that they may just have signed the next Wayne Rooney when in fact they may have just signed the next Wayne Sleep but it's a gamble the manufacturers just have to take.

Increasingly, the top brands, particularly Nike, are muscling in like never before. You got a sense of the kind of sway that these companies now have at the 1998 World Cup Final when Ronaldo, injured and out of the final against France, was propelled back into the starting line-up allegedly because Nike wanted Brazil's star player – their star player – in the biggest game there is wearing their shirts. Whether it is true or not, I have absolutely no idea but it's worrying to think that the manufacturers could actually wield that kind of influence.

There's even an ongoing struggle for which ball is used in the big leagues yet there was a time not so long ago when every team used to play with a white Mitre ball (or an orange one if the weather turned nasty). Nowadays, you've got Nike as the official Premiership ball, Adidas as the provider of the World Cup ball and the Champions League and poor old Mitre are left with the FA Cup.

Inevitably, though, there is a conflict of interests between the players, the clubs and the manufacturers. Now I'm not one to start conspiracy theories (well maybe I am) but look at the case of David Beckham. For years, Beckham had been the main man at Adidas and while Umbro made Man Utd's kit, it didn't seem to be that much of a problem. But when United switched shirts to Nike, Beckham was out and on his way to Real Madrid, an Adidas club. Was that because Nike didn't want their main rival's biggest asset at 'their' club? Of course not, but I like to start ridiculous rumours. Then again, he has just gone to Major League Soccer, which is owned by . . . Adidas.

It's the same with Wayne Rooney. When he moved to Nike United he did so having just signed a massive long-term boot deal with, yep, you've guessed it, Nike. Coincidence? Well, yes it is actually. I made both of the above up. Good though aren't they?

Whether you choose to believe these conspiracy theories is up to you but I love the Nike and Adidas battle and there can be only one winner – football.

EPILOGUE

WHAT I STILL HAVE TO DO TO BECOME THE BIGGEST FAN IN THE WORLD

Football has been, and still is, an enormous part of my life. When I started writing the book, though, I secretly worried that I was a rubbish football fan. If anything I now think I may well be the BIGGEST FAN IN THE WORLD.

Look at the facts: I have played and watched football all my life; I have followed my team all over the country; I have had the opportunity to meet and forge friendships with innumerable players; I have played football with genuine legends of the game at some of the most historic stadiums in the world; I've worked in television, radio and in magazines talking about football; I write a regular piece in the Chelsea matchday programme; I'm now presenting the football phone-in institution that is Radio Five Live's 6–0–6 and, finally, I'm one of the few people that's not a professional player to have made a living out of the game. In my mind I might be the biggest fan in the world now, but I'd like to reassure you that, in truth, I'm no better than you. No man can be a bigger or better fan than any other. It's a game for all the people. I have, however, set myself a list of things I simply have to do in football before I die . . .

1 I HAVE TO SEE ENGLAND WIN THE WORLD CUP

I think that seeing your national team win the world cup must be the most unbelievable experience. I feel really jealous of those people that were around in 1966 who saw England do it and got to sing clever, imaginative songs like:

We won the cup!
We won the cup!
Ee-aye-adio
We won the cup!

That's brilliant. I do believe, however, that it would better if we didn't win it on British soil, because if you can do it in foreign climes then the achievement is so much greater. The problem for England is that the World Cup is always played in the summer, which is really bad timing for the British players. Not only are they tired after a long season but they end up playing in ridiculous temperatures, losing half their body weight during the games and running out of steam by the quarter-finals. No wonder Brazil and the South Americans always do well. They're used to playing in 30 degrees plus.

I've always thought that the timing of the World Cup should change every four years, just to make things fairer. One year it should be a summer tournament and the next time round it should be played in the middle of our winter. Let's see Ronaldinho do his tricks when it's −3 or the pitch is waterlogged and there's mud up to his knees.

The big chance we do have is when the World Cup goes to South Africa in 2010 because while it is in the middle of our summer it's actually in the middle of their winter down there. Hopefully, it'll rain too which means we revert to type. That means percentage football where we just hoof it up to a big striker and make the most of our rich tradition of playing the long ball game. In fact, we should just take a squad of long ball specialists. Big centre-halves, big strikers, no fancy-dans. Just hit the channels. It won't be pretty but we could go far.

2 I NEED TO WATCH A FOOTBALL MATCH IN EVERY CONTINENT

I've been trying for years to get to South America to see a game and now, following my retirement from *Soccer AM* and with a little more time on my hands, I'm planning on getting on a plane to Argentina and taking in a Boca Juniors or River Plate game in the very near future. It's just one of those experiences that you can't miss out on. Asia fascinates me too. Countries like South Korea and China have all taken football to their heart and I would dearly love to experience their take on the game. As for Japan, just have a look around YouTube at their fans and tell me they are not the best on the planet. They've taken the best elements from every other football nation and created an atmosphere unlike anything else. It is loud, passionate and colourful and their singing p****s all over everyone else in the world.

3 I HAVE TO MEET PELE AND MARADONA

I have met many legendary footballers throughout the course of my career but it will mean nothing in my quest to become the world's biggest fan unless I get to meet Pele and Maradona. Apparently, 'The Great Pele' as he is always called, often needs an incentive if he's going to give you an audience so I'm saving as we speak. Many moons ago, we came close to doing a piece with Maradona on *Soccer AM*. We had been given a number to call and when we did some bloke answered who claimed he represented Diego. He then told us that if we were going to interview him they would want cash upfront before we flew over. To be honest, it all sounded a bit dodgy so rather than send one of the team half way across the world on a wild goose chase we decided not to bother.

4 I HAVE TO FATHER A SON WHO CAN PLAY PROFESSIONALLY

While I may have slipped through the net, I feel there that I need to pass my talented genes on to a boy who can go on to play professional football. Now I'm no longer married, I need to choose the next mother of my children carefully. She needs to be sporty, to be able to run fast and to jump high. I may even get her on the stopwatch round the local park before we take the relationship any further. I'm not being picky but if I am going to maximise the chance of fathering a future Premier League player, I will need to know the mother's pedigree.

For a dad to see their son play professional football must be the next best thing to actually playing. I never really wanted a son when me and my ex-wife thought about kids and in the end I got myself twin daughters but I fancy a son now, not to carry on the name or the bloodline or anything silly like that but to inherit the Lovejoy football legacy. I wouldn't even mind if he played for Spurs as long as he got a run-out for England.

5 I HAVE TO OWN MY OWN FOOTBALL CLUB

It strikes me that the ultimate commitment to football is either owning your own club or at the very least, sitting on the board. Personally, I already own a square centimetre of the pitch at Stamford Bridge through the Chelsea Pitch Owners scheme. It was bought for me as a present by Helen Chamberlain and while they don't actually allocate you a specific section of the pitch, I like to think that my little bit is just outside the box at the Shed end. Technically speaking, I think I may even be within my right to prosecute opposition players for trespass if they venture on to my piece of grass.

To be a real fan, though, I need to extend that square centimetre of turf to owning my own football club. It's a big ask and I imagine I'll have to look at a non-league club. Maybe Chorleywood Under-18s?

But that would be ultimate dream: to have enough cash to invest in a football club. As a fan there is nothing more you can do because, unless you own Man Utd or Liverpool, there really is no money to be made out of a football club. It's like going to a casino. You just need to go there knowing how much you're prepared to lose and stick to it. Eventually, when I've made my millions, billions or gazillions, or however much I make, I'm going to go and see Roman Abramovich and make him an offer he can't refuse. After all, I've already got a bit of the pitch so I'm half way there . . .

Writing this book has proved to be an extremely therapeutic process. I realize that football is like quicksand. I just seem to get deeper and deeper into the game. And the older I get, the more I am convinced that everybody loves football…it's just that some people don't know it yet. And everyone should open their heart to the beautiful game and let it into their life.

This is my first book, and I hope it's a success and maybe wins some new fans over to the most important subject in the world. In fact, I hope it turns out like Razor Ruddock's underpants:

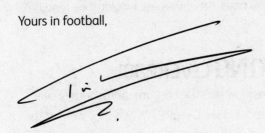

HUGE

Yours in football,

Timothy P. Lovejoy

EXTRAS

During the course of writing this book I found that there was some material that I couldn't quite place in any of the chapters.

In the modern era, where we all want something extra for free, I thought it only right to package up these random thoughts, tidy them up and put them in this new 'hidden' extras chapter at the back of the book, just like they do with DVDs. If you've managed to find it (obviously you have, otherwise you wouldn't be reading this), well done.

BORING **BORING** LIVERPOOL

Changing the back pass law was the best amendment they ever introduced to the rulebook. Take Liverpool. When they were at the height of their success they would go 1-0 up and then it was just Clemence to Thompson to Clemence to Neal to Clemence to Hansen to Clemence to Kennedy to Clemence to Dalglish, a bit of magic, Rush slots it home, then back to Clemence to Thompson to Clemence to Neal . . . until the final whistle went. Thankfully, the back pass law put an end to all that business of rolling it back to the keeper who would then pick it up, bounce it a few times and then roll out to the full back.

★ ★ ★ ★

Why is injury time in the second half of a game always longer than in the first half, irrespective of the actual number of stoppages in each half?

Why is it that whenever a goalkeeper plays well, the opposition fans say 'If it wasn't for their keeper, we'd have walked that game?' You never hear, 'If their striker hadn't have scored a hat-trick we'd have won that match 3–1' do you?

★ ★ ★ ★

UP FOR THE CUP(S)

In my eyes, the most iconic trophy there is is the World Cup and, what's more, I have lifted it. Well, I say I've lifted it but what I actually lifted was one of the many replicas that FIFA send out around the world. You see, your chance of getting anywhere close to the real one are virtually nil; Sepp Blatter keeps that one under lock and key.

Sorry to disappoint anyone but there are a handful of FA Cups that travel round the country too. There's the original one with dents, bruises and the impressions of team captain's lips on it that the Football Association keep a keen eye on. Then there's the shiny replicas which crop up in TV studios and in photo-opportunities as and when needed. Sad but true.

There is a theory that holds that a trophy is not a real trophy unless it has handles, like the European Cup. I don't buy that. Look at the Ashes urn. You can barely see that, yet alone lift it above your head and yet that is one of the most recognisable trophies of all. It's the same with the World Cup. Lifting that 14 inches of 18-carat gold, even if it was a replica and even if it didn't have handles, was a great experience. It was a lovely feeling holding it in the air.

THE CAMERA **NEVER** LIES

Sky has undeniably revolutionised the way we watch the national game. More live games, more analysis, scores more cameras, Fanzone, Player-Cam, the list goes on. But there's one trick they've missed and it has to change.

Let me explain. When I go to Chelsea matches, I'm fortunate enough to sit just behind the dugout so I always get a great view of Jose Mourinho and the opposition manager tearing their hair out as the game progresses. With that in mind, it occurred to me that the managers are often as entertaining as the actual football these days. They are tacticians and motivators, coaches and confidantes.

So let me reveal my latest idea: Manager-Cam. Essentially, it's cameras set up to focus exclusively on the coaches as they do all those complicated hand signals they always do or scream instructions at their players. This should take the form of a small square in the corner of your screen which doesn't interfere with play but allows you to watch them for ninety minutes.

★ ★ ★ ★

COME ON THE FORCES!

I always tried to look after the Armed Forces on *Soccer AM*. In the last decade or so there's been a variety of conflicts around the world and regardless of whether you agree with them or not, you should never really forget that the forces are the ones who have been brave enough to go out there and fight on our behalf. So while other TV programmes may feature the forces as and when it suits them, I made a point of keeping them in the public eye simply because they deserve it.

The funniest thing the forces do is that whenever they go on the tours abroad to Iraq, Afghanistan or wherever, the first thing they seem to pack is their club's shirt. Each week, we would receive these incredible pictures of someone standing in the desert or on top of a tank with a Plymouth Argyle or a Shrewsbury shirt on. Towards the end of my time at *Soccer AM* we also got letters from families whose relatives had been featured on the show but who had since been killed in action.

That's why I tried to do a little bit for them. That's why I always say 'Come On The Forces!'

Why, when it's not politically correct to point out if someone is short, obese or has disabilities, is it acceptable to question Peter Crouch's ability as a player based purely on his height?

Why do referees always blow the final whistle when the ball is in mid-air following a goal kick?

Why are attacking left-footed players always called 'wizards' when they're right-footed counterparts get no such compliment? Also, why is it that slow players are always called 'intelligent' players?

DEFENDERS ARE CHEATS

What bugs me more than anything about the modern offside law is defenders moaning about it. Under the old offside law, the back four (usually Arsenal's) always used to step up as one with their hands in the air to catch the strikers offside. Now you have defenders complaining that the forwards are cheating when they wander around in offside position before running back towards their own goal and then turn around and join in the attack again. It's not in the spirit of the game, they say. But surely walking up in a sneaky way, trying to set the offside trap, was *not* in the spirit of the game, and clearly cheating.

Why, when a young English manager has a string of good results at club level, is he instantly earmarked as the next manager of the national team?

Whatever happened to indirect free-kicks? Nobody ever seems to get them these days . . .

WHAT DO FANS BRING TO THE GAME?

I don't like to knock fans as we all have our different ways of watching the matches. My brother used to get agitated and angry, whereas I'm a little more mellow. However it's now 2008 and I'm still watching football matches in which footballers who are about take throw-ins and corners only to find mindless morons hanging over the fences, shouting, swearing and doing hand signals at them.

Am I the only one who's finding this just a little tiresome now? Maybe when we're discussing using video footage against players after matches we should be able to also use it to throw out these idiots?

Isn't it about time we all just grew up a bit? When you look at these people, they're grown men acting like 14-year-olds and behaving like Neanderthals.

As paying fans, you should be able to have banter and criticise as much as you like, but to stand up and make obscene gestures seems a little outdated.

★ ★ ★ ★

Premier League managers wanting to look like tactical geniuses have to spend the first half of the match watching from the stands, only moving to the dugout if things start to go wrong on the pitch.

YOU ARE **THE JEFF**

I really don't know who came up with idea of Sky's *Soccer Saturday* but whoever it was is an absolute genius. The idea of a load of blokes sitting watching a match that the viewer can't see seems like television madness but it's actually quite compelling and the magic ingredient is Jeff Stelling. He makes the show.

There was a time when we all used to sit round watching Teletext or Oracle waiting for the scores to flash up or you'd listen to the radio. The trouble then was that the results never came through quick enough. Suddenly, *Soccer Saturday* came along and you had so much information on the screen with ticker tapes, people being sent off, what penalty's being missed. Fantastic. Try to explain to a wife or girlfriend who doesn't appreciate football that you're being entertained by watching a load of blokes watching football matches that you can't even see. The person who keeps it all together is Jeff.

What he has done on that show is nothing short of incredible. Remember, this is SIX HOURS of live television, with scores and results flying in from all round the country and with information being fed to him every single second. How he manages to do it is astonishing. That he does it every week is a testament to his professionalism. That he manages to do it with a fantastic sense of humour too is just brilliant. He has had a couple of crackers over the years. I remember when news of Guyain Nduma-nsunga scoring for Sheffield Wednesday came through to him he came out with 'Local boy makes good' and whenever the Welsh team Total Network Solutions won a game he'd say 'they'll be dancing on the streets of Total Network Solutions tonight . . .'

When a player comes to the bench for a drink from a water bottle, he has to spit the first mouthful all over the pitch before actually having a drink.

If at any point a player kicks a ball onto a roof or over a stand, the crowd have to cheer loudly.

ROBBIE **NOSE** BEST

There's been a lot of fashions amongst footballers, like slogan t-shirts, bleached hair, beards, and Vicks on your shirt. But by far the weirdest is nasal strips. Remember them? They were like a little plaster that went across the bridge of the nose and were meant to enlarge the nostrils and increase the flow of air to the lungs. I think. Robbie persevered with them for longer than just about anybody else in the game. I asked him once why he wore them and he told me he really thought it helped him. The only slight snag is, when you're out of breath you actually breathe through your mouth, so they're of no practical use at all. But I'll wait till I'm as good as Robbie Fowler before I criticize his choice of nosewear.

Why do newspapers start printing the league tables after the first week of the season? Don't managers have enough pressure on them already?

Why are the penalty box and six-yard box rectangular and not semi-circular?

Why, when a player scores two goals in a game do reporters always say that they've 'bagged a brace' when this word is never, ever used in everyday English?

★ ★ ★ ★

YOU **DA** MANI!

Can't do a book without mentioning Mani, the Manc Messiah as we called him, the bass player with Primal Scream and the people's poet. Mani is just an absolute hero of mine. He was always up for coming on the show, sometimes at the drop of a hat. When a guest we had lined up pulled out at the last moment, we gave Mani a call in Manchester, asked him if he was available and told him that there might a few quid in it for him. 'No worries,' he said. 'I'll jump on a train and come down and help you boys out. You've been good to me so I'll be good to you. I might as well 'cos I need to buy a new carpet.' You can't argue with that kind of logic; I need a new carpet so I'll go on *Soccer AM*. I've said it before, but I really believe Mani should be the godfather to every child that's born. He's a top man.

Why, when central defenders score, do they have no idea how to celebrate?

PRESTON **DEAD** END

Preston is a top bloke but I really worry about people who can't kick a ball properly. What were they doing while we were all growing up and kicking balls around the playground? Over the years, we had countless celebrities try their luck on the shoot-out game at the end of *Soccer AM* but I can categorically say that Preston, lead singer with The Ordinary Boys, is by far the worst person I have ever seen kick a ball, or rather attempt to kick a ball.

Many guests have confessed that they're not very good at football but have nevertheless managed to get the ball heading in the general direction of the target. Poor Preston couldn't even do that. It just seemed like there was no communication between his brain and his legs. Thankfully he doesn't need his legs to play the guitar and sing.

If the home defender heads the ball back to his own goalkeeper, allowing him to pick the ball up, it has to draw an over-generous round of applause from the crowd.

When you're team's knocked out of a Cup, it's automatically known as the 'Mickey Mouse Cup', especially when it comes to Premier League teams and the Carling Cup

FACE THE MUSIC

The link between football and music is a strange one, linked only by the fans themselves. For a start, the footballers have no idea about any guitar bands simply because all they like is R&B and MTV Base yet all the people in bands still tend to like football. And then you have the fans in the middle who happen to like both music and football. But still before the games, all you'll hear blaring out of the team dressing room is R&B, rather than what the rest of the country is listening to. Why is that?

There are so many celebrity footballers now who turn up at charity games having claimed to have had 'trials' at some club or other when they were younger then when the game kicks off it's patently obvious that the only trials they've been to was either at the local Magistrate's Court or at Badminton.

It used to be our little joke on *Soccer AM* that whenever anybody mentioned that they had had trials we all used to shout 'We've all had trials, we've all had trials for someone.' And it's true. By my reckoning, everyone in the known world must have had a trial for some club or other at some stage. It doesn't mean they were any good.

If a team wins a semi-final or a final, they have to line up holding hands, before running towards their fans and simultaneously diving on the floor. Nobody knows why.

★ ★ ★ ★

WHITE SOCKS

I have a theory that all the best teams play in white socks, and as a player I was only ever happy playing in white socks myself. I am not alone in this and I understand it's a psychological issue for a lot of players. I remember Ruud Gullit signing for Chelsea and saying he had a good feeling about playing for the Blues as they played in white socks. When he became manager of Newcastle the team changed their traditional black socks to white for a season. My reckoning is that white socks make you feel more skilful. Often if teams have dark socks you will see players either taping their ankles with white tape or wearing white ankle socks in order to give them a mental edge going into a game.

It's amazing the effect a football kit can have on a player, both Stuart Pearce and Paolo Di Canio like to wear their shorts short so they could see their thighs. Di Canio said it empowered him.

Back to socks. I understand from my friends who play rugby that wearing white socks was always a bad thing as it didn't make you feel strong and tough going into a maul. However, the recent England rugby kit has got white socks for the first time. Does this mean they'll be playing with flair or will they be chickening out of the tackles? The final note on white socks is look at all the great teams who wear them: Chelsea, Brazil, Milan, Ajax, Real Madrid, Juventus, Germany, England, Lazio . . .

Whenever a vacant manager's job becomes available, David O'Leary's management company has to immediately rule him out of contention.

★ ★ ★ ★

CARBON BOOTPRINT

Something about European football has been bugging me for quite a while now. I'm concerned that Europe's premier club competition is not good for the environment, and can only be a matter of time before the 'right-on' Green brigade get their teeth stuck right into it.

The problem with the Champions League as far as the environment goes is that each match sees thousands of people flying across the continent twice in the space of 24 hours – If

Manchester United are playing away to Roma, then one flight will carry all their players and club officials while several others will take their thousands of followers to the Italian capital for the sake of watching 90 minutes of football.

Now you or I will know that this is an extremely worthwhile use of air fuel, but I'm a bit shocked the environmental activists haven't already been campaigning to stop European football or for that matter international friendly matches due to the huge carbon footprint football's leaving.

With football being such an easy target, I'm genuinely surprised that this hasn't already happened.

These days, when Premier League teams travel across the country for a league match they tend to fly so will there be a time in the future when the FA will have to arrange away games as road trips?

For example, Liverpool would have to play West Ham, Chelsea, Spurs and Arsenal all in the space of a month, and be based in London throughout, so they don't wreck the environment by jetting to and from Merseyside for each match.

Will we get to a stage where the cup competitions have to be divided into northern and southern sections to save the planet (as already happens in the early rounds of the Carling Cup and Johnstone's Paint Trophy)?

I really hope I haven't opened up a terrible can of worms by writing this. If you are Al Gore, please ignore everything I've just written

★ ★ ★ ★

After half-time at the new Wembley, John Motson has to spend the first ten minutes of the second half preoccupied with when the corporate ticket-holders will be back to their seats.

★ ★ ★ ★

LITTLE WONDERS

There is a general rule of thumb in sport that the bigger and stronger you are the more likely you are to succeed. Basketball, tennis, rugby, even golf; if you're high and mighty you're going to have a massive advantage.

But it's not quite the same in football. Look at the evidence. Some of the greatest players in history have been vertically challenged: Diego Maradona, Gianfranco Zola, Juninho, Deco, Romario. Even the current World Player of the Year, Fabio Cannavaro, is barely 5ft 8in. My personal favourite of the little guys, though, has to be Lionel 'Leo' Messi. At 5t 7in and slight of frame, the Argentinian is one of the undisputed stars of the world game now and is capable of scoring some of the most amazing individual goals despite, or maybe even because of his compact size. Witness that goal he scored for Barcelona against Getafe this year. It was like Maradona in his prime. He may be small but he's a giant of a man in my eyes.

The flip side, though, is that football also affords opportunities to those players who are also carrying a bit of lumber. Jan Molby, Ivan Campo, Mick Quinn and even Gazza have all taken to the pitch looking like they've had one too many trips to the sweet trolley. But has it affected them? Of course it hasn't.

AND ANOTHER THING ...

Why is it '... and Leicester' during the middle of the 'Over Land And Sea' song? Surely there are other teams' names that scan just as well?

TEAMS ARE NEVER 'TOO GOOD TO GO DOWN'

Why do people always say that teams are 'too good to go down'? I've said it before and I'll say it again, the best team always wins the league title and the worst three teams always go down. Fact.

HOW TO ADDRESS THE GUNNERS

Here's a question for you. Why it is only The Arsenal that gets to have the definitive article preceding their club name. It doesn't happen with any other club I can think of. The Liverpool? No. The Manchester United? Nope. The Grimsby? ...

AND FINALLY ...

Whose idea was it to put advertising on a ref? I'm certainly not flying Air Asia.

Goodbye ...